T0195724

Complexity
and Paradox

Jim Underwood

STRATEGY

03.05

■ Fast track route to mastering highly complex environments

■ Covers the fundamentals of complexity management, from
encouraging iconoclastic behavior and setting up formal
complexity training to using scenarios and gathering
intelligence

■ Examples and lessons from some of the world's most
sophisticated businesses, including Microsoft, and ideas from
the smartest thinkers including H. Igor Ansoff, Richard A
D'Aveni and Peter Schwartz

■ Includes a glossary of key concepts and a comprehensive
resources guide

>>EXPRESS EXEC.COM<<

essential management thinking at your fingertips

First published 2002 by
Capstone Publishing (a Wiley company)
8 Newtec Place
Magdalen Road
Oxford OX4 1RE
United Kingdom
http://www.capstoneideas.com

CIP catalogue records for this book are available from the British Library and the US Library of Congress

ISBN 1-84112-225-4

This book is printed on acid-free paper

Substantial discounts on bulk quantities of Capstone books are available to corporations, professional associations and other organizations. Please contact Capstone for more details on +44 (0)1865 798 623 or (fax) +44 (0)1865 240 941 or (e-mail) info@wiley-capstone.co.uk

Contents

Introduction to ExpressExec

ExpressExec is 3 million words of the latest management thinking compiled into 10 modules. Each module contains 10 individual titles forming a comprehensive resource of current business practice written by leading practitioners in their field. From brand management to balanced scorecard, ExpressExec enables you to grasp the key concepts behind each subject and implement the theory immediately. Each of the 100 titles is available in print and electronic formats.

Through the ExpressExec.com Website you will discover that you can access the complete resource in a number of ways:

» printed books or e-books;
» e-content – PDF or XML (for licensed syndication) adding value to an intranet or Internet site;
» a corporate e-learning/knowledge management solution providing a cost-effective platform for developing skills and sharing knowledge within an organization;
» bespoke delivery – tailored solutions to solve your need.

Why not visit www.expressexec.com and register for free key management briefings, a monthly newsletter and interactive skills checklists. Share your ideas about ExpressExec and your thoughts about business today.

Please contact elound@wiley-capstone.co.uk for more information.

Introduction to Complexity and Paradox

The first chapter explains why complexity is so important to managers in the twenty-first century.

Complexity: the nonlinear or unpredictable interaction of systems within the global system in which there are still elements of predictability.

There are a lot of people out there writing highly technical academic articles about complexity who are a lot more knowledgeable about the subject than I am. So why in the world would a strategist write a book about complexity?

The answer to the question is "balance." The field of complexity is penetrating every aspect of management, as well as strategy theory. A number of people are suggesting that the basic constructs of complexity theory must be metaphorically applied to the application of strategy and management theory. That is, the real world. In my opinion, this is true. There is a place for complexity theory and chaos theory in the fields of management and strategy. In fact, I wrote a book (*Thriving in E-Chaos*, Prima Publishers, Roseville, CA, 2001) that blended complexity theory and strategy. So what's the problem?

First, the average article about complexity theory is often so technical that it fails to connect with the manager who is trying to develop a corporate strategic plan for next year. Second, most articles (and many books that focus upon complexity theory as a basis for management and strategy) make a number of assumptions that are simply not well founded.

That is why a strategist (me) is writing a book about complexity theory. First, complexity theory does not have to be overrun with an entirely new, massive, and confusing vocabulary. That is just not necessary. Second, before blindly accepting some of the assumptions that are the foundation of many current applications of complexity theory, it might be helpful for the manager if he or she understood how those assumptions were developed. In fact, once the manager understands the fallacious nature of some of those metaphorical assumptions, it is quite probable that the application of complexity theory, and its first cousin, "self-organizing companies", will be seen with a less positive view.

That is the issue: balance. Managers need to (and deserve to) understand all of the assumptions that underlie an approach. If, in fact, those assumptions have problems, they need to know that as well.

There is one other thing that the reader needs to understand at this point: complexity (and chaos) theory has an important place in strategic and management thinking. The idea of complex systems (and complex organizations) may be one of the most important concepts that the manager of the twenty-first century needs to understand. In fact, managers who are able to think in terms of complexity and apply that to the competitive environment will probably lead higher performing organizations than will their counterparts who do not think in that way.

ANOTHER COMPLEXITY ISSUE

In my opinion, complexity (as well as chaos, and environmental rate of change) is the "phantom" issue in many (if not most) of the management books that have been published over the past 20 years. Many of the books on quality, change, change management, process re-engineering, etc. have been written in response to the problems that companies have been having in dealing with complexity. (In many cases, the solution was ill-founded since it did not address the problem, but the book was still written with the purpose of trying to explain the deterioration of corporate profits.)

Regardless, complexity, chaos, and environmental change are important issues for the manager of the 2000s. In fact, they may be the key to understanding how to maximize corporate profits.

It is my objective to help managers understand the role that complexity plays in every decision they make. Further, once understood in its proper context, the application of complexity theory may become one of the most important tools in the manager's arsenal of solutions.

THE BASICS

Everyone who has been on a diet understands that there is more to the food we eat than is shown on the label. For example, a food labeled "fat free" can be loaded with sugar. The unsuspecting diet-conscious person might choose a particular food because it is advertised as being healthy, when in fact it is not.

The same is true of the topic of complexity. A lot of recent books are founded upon the idea of complexity, but there is a lot more to the authors' ideas than meets the eye. Additionally, there are issues related to complexity that a number of recent works have not addressed.

The idea of complexity has its roots in natural science, physics, and mathematics. Throughout history, those studying natural phenomena have debated the mystery that surrounds the physical events of nature. That is where the paradox begins. On one hand, if one decides to put a drop of dye into a glass of water, the chaotic nature of the water molecules means that the diffusion of the dye in the water will be unpredictable. One time, for instance, it might go straight to the bottom of the glass, while on another occasion it might diffuse across the surface of the water first.

The mystery is that one drop of dye in a glass of water will always turn the water a specific color. In spite of the chaotic nature of the diffusion of the dye, the outcome will always be the same. That is just one of the paradoxes that exist in creation. There are many more.

COMPLEXITY AND THE BUSINESS WORLD

For a number of decades, business theorists have attempted to establish a link between complexity and chaos in the natural world and the apparent complexity and chaos in the business world. This topic became especially meaningful during the 1980s and 1990s as Japanese companies appeared to be poised to control world commerce before just as quickly fading from the forefront. Then the technology revolution arrived and many thought it was the epitome of a chaotic, complex world. The emergence of the topsy-turvy environment of the new century convinced many that complexity and chaos would certainly characterize the global market for years to come.

The major driving force behind the business theorists' interest in complexity may have had something to do with the degree of difficulty that business managers were having in dealing with change. Out of those challenges came ideas about "systems thinking" and "change management." In the end, however, it became apparent that no one idea or practice was going to provide the final solution for business managers. It is obvious that complex situations require complex solutions.

The real issue regarding complexity has to do with how these ideas can be used to maximize organizational profit. The question has a number of answers. First, it is important to realize that there are some theories out there that have little, if any, support in the real world of business. Second, a number of these theories are founded upon supposed scientific "fact" that has much more to do with faith than fact. Finally, some of the conclusions reached by such theorists (such as "self-organization") are problematic at best.

My objective in this book is to introduce the reader to the various ideas about complexity that have been proposed over the past few years, and to critically react with some of them to offer the reader a logical critique of some of those hypotheses.

In addition, I will propose a number of solutions to the complexity problem that will enable the business manager more effectively to carve profit out of complexity and chaos.

Complexity Theory: Key Terms and Definitions

This chapter investigates many of the most commonly used terms and ideas in the field.

WHAT IS COMPLEXITY THEORY?

Complexity theory has its roots in many disciplines. Basically, it has been the result of efforts by "thinkers" who want to explain the "why" and the "how" of processes. Charles Darwin's hypothesis of evolution is just such an attempt to explain the whole of existence.

Generally, most of those who work in the field of complexity assume or promote an atheistic view of creation (i.e. there is no God, or creator, nor has there ever been one). In some ways it is possible to conclude that much of the work done in the field has been approached with the idea of disproving a theistic view of the origin of existence.

At the same time, both views seem to run a parallel course. Evolutionists believe that the complex system that has evolved to what it is today (all of existence) began with a "big bang." No mention is made of what created the matter and energy that allowed this random event to occur, however. At the heart of the idea of evolution is a "miracle" (creation) without a cause. Further, the evolutionist would suggest that the world is constantly evolving from simplicity to complexity as well as from a state of inferior to superior (a continual dynamic of improvement).

Theism (in this case the Judeo-Christian view is offered) suggests that the original creation began with complexity. That is, an original, uncaused cause (God) created existence in an original state of complexity.

Both views assume some level of order. The theist assumes that the global system (including nature) continues to work upon a created heuristic. The theist would argue, for example (as Darwin also pointed out), that we see no evolution from one species (or kind) to another. That is, we have no evidence that a frog has ever become a prince. The evolutionist argues for the upward spiral of increasing complexity, and therefore assumes that evolutionary jumps between kinds is reality. In the 1980s there was a televised debate between two eminent scientists. One was a respected evolutionist, and the other a creationist. The evolutionist affirmed that there was no evidence to support the Darwinian hypothesis. He further stated that he believed it would be found some day.

There is a third view that needs to be considered in this debate. That view is that complexity theory need not necessarily presuppose a

Darwinian metaphor. In fact, that presupposition may be an obstacle to dealing with complexity.

The one thing that all camps should be able to agree on is that complexity is reality. In addition, the chaotic interaction of systems in a complex macro system results in events that are unpredictable.

While many phenomena are linear in nature, and appear to have always been such (in natural science, for example), there are systems that are clearly nonlinear. Generally speaking, those tend to be social systems and economic systems. Certainly, the environment has aspects of complexity and unpredictability, but at the same time it appears that the global system we call the environment operates with linear heuristics as its foundation. That brings us to a critical point in the consideration of complexity theory.

If we shed the presuppositions that separate both schools, we end up with a new and more realistic understanding of systems.

1 Some aspects of the global system (all of existence) are complex and unpredictable.
2 Some aspects of the global system are linear.
3 In both nature and in social systems (defined here to include societal, business, economic, etc.) there are aspects of those systems that are complex and unpredictable.

Therefore, we end up with an opportunity to use complexity theory in a way that is uninhibited by unsubstantiated constructs. That is, complexity may be defined as the nonlinear or unpredictable inter-action of systems within the global system in which there are still elements of predictability. Further, the apparently random interaction between those systems may reveal certain understandable and ulti-mately predictable outcomes, at least as to the nature of the emerging system.

What this means for the business manager is that the observable complexity of the global system is reality. At the same time, it is possible to anticipate the nature of outcomes related to the interaction of those systems. This does not mean that specific events can be predicted but that in some cases they can. More importantly, however, it means that by observing the macroenvironment it is possible for the manager to begin to make certain reliable inferences about the outcomes of the interaction of those systems. Additionally, it means that the manager is not "bound" by a presupposition that is founded in a false heuristic (the Darwinian hypothesis) but rather can consider such complexity in a more predictive paradigm.

GLOSSARY FOR COMPLEXITY THEORY[1]

The following definitions are quoted from Amanda Corcoran's work in which she did an excellent job of synthesizing the work of numerous sources. For more information, go to the Website shown in the reference area.

» **Agents/elements**: individual autocatalytic elements' interaction within a system or community.
» **Autocatalytic**: independent actions of elements within a system resulting (hopefully) in change to self and to system (auto: self; catalytic: inspiring change).
» **Bifurcation**: to divide into two parts.
» **Butterfly effect**: small variables effect large changes within a system; chaos theory, edge of chaos.
» **Community**: group sharing common characteristics or interests.
» **Complex**: intricate association of individual parts forming a whole.
» **Complexity theory**: theory, based upon chaos theory, that evolution occurs most effectively through interaction.
» **Edge of chaos**: point between chaos and stasis where evolution is most likely to occur.
» **Elements**: independent entities within a system.
» **Emergent properties**: properties or characteristics directly resulting from interactions within or between complex systems and environments, e.g. knowledge.
» **Interactions**: behaviors and communications occurring in direct reaction with other elements, systems, or environments.
» **Reaction**: to act in response to an agent, influence, or stimulus.
» **Strange attractors**: areas around which behaviors and interactions tend to occur.
» **System**: unified whole of different independently acting entities.

NOTE

1. http://www.arc.losrios.cc.ca.us/~corcora/complg.html (Exact quotes taken from the Web page.)

The Evolution of Complexity and Chaos Thinking

This chapter explains the problems related to previous theories of management. It also develops ideas for managing in complex environments.

The evolution of thinking about complexity is a reflection of the field itself. The struggle to explain existence is inseparably linked to many theorists' attempts to explain complexity in the organizational setting. On one hand, the reality of complexity in the business environment is obvious. On the other, attempts to explain complexity are not so simple.

The various disciplines are replete with instances where a concept is developed within a discipline only to be borrowed by another. Complexity and chaos are two such areas. While the concepts originated in the natural sciences, related concepts have been found in such diverse fields as theology and business management.

The equilibrium theory of economics has its roots in the late 1800s. At the heart of the theory is the idea of linearity or rationality. That is, the economic system (according to one view) is composed of a grouping of significant forces that lend themselves to linear or predictable behavior. Much of the thinking that underlies the approach is based upon the presuppositions that even though systems change, they will normally change in fairly predictable ways.

Out of that thinking came many of the management theories of the early 1900s. Again, the idea was to take a concept developed for one discipline (in this case microeconomics) and metaphorically use it as a basis for explaining another (such as business management). Since the equilibrium metaphor was linear in nature, those who adapted it to management theory also presupposed linearity into all of their thinking.

Early mental models in the field of strategy were generally limited to such ideas. In fact, most corporate planning has historically focused on the budgeting process. In many cases, executives will admit that even today, the strategy process often has little to do with how assets are allocated. Further, many will admit that the budgeting process, and the linear extension of historical trends, is really the basis for the strategy/budgeting process.

In the early 1940s, a few people began to ask about complexity theory and how it might metaphorically apply to the business management field.[1] With the apparent failure of the linear-based budgeting approach in the 1960s and 1970s, the search for new ways to think about managing and planning began to intensify. George Steiner's 1963 book *Managerial Long-range Planning* (McGraw-Hill) introduced the idea of separating financial and strategic planning. Another concept introduced in the book was that of corporate self-determination. Basically, what a number of contributors to Steiner's book suggested was that companies needed to develop a strategic plan for future initiatives, and in turn the strategic plan should then drive the budgeting process.[2]

H. Igor Ansoff's first book, *Corporate Strategy*, was introduced at about the same time.[3] Ansoff was apparently intrigued by the extremely complex nature of organizations. On one hand, he appears to have adopted the equilibrium theory-based paradigm of "competitive advantage." On the other, a careful reading of the book reveals a highly complex and somewhat adaptive approach to strategy. By 1990, Ansoff had revised his 1963 book and it was titled *The New Corporate Strategy*.[4] In this book it was clear that the entire tone and direction of Ansoff's work had changed completely. The revision produced a book that was clearly founded in cybernetics, systems thinking, and complexity theory.

While Ansoff's objective was to keep *The New Corporate Strategy* extremely user-friendly, the same was not true of his 1986 book *Implanting Strategic Management*. Notice how he handles the complexity adaptiveness issues in talking about the "firm of the future."

> "The growing reliance on complex decision support systems will necessitate greater rapport between staff management analysts and line managers. The size, complexity, and diversity of the firm will lead to further decentralization of decision making. Thus, as the firm becomes a more complex information system, it also becomes a complex behavioral system with diverse aspirations, values, norms, and cultures."[5]

By that time Ansoff's thinking had moved from an equilibrium-based view of the environment (as well as the firm) to a complex, adaptive, systems-based view. (Actually he adopted a complex dynamic view of the environment. The differences between the two will be discussed later in this book.) At the same time, he recognized the critical links that exist between the complex system called the environment and the requisite complex adaptiveness that the firm would have to possess if it were to effectively deal with changing environments.

The confusion created by the rapidly changing "rules of the game" of the 1980s produced a number of new ideas as a result of the cognitive dissonance related to the core competencies, equilibrium-based strategic approach. It was during this time that total quality management began to gain widespread acceptance, to be followed by process re-engineering. (For an excellent look at this issue, see "Time – the next source of competitive advantage" in the *Harvard Business Review*, July-August 1988.) At best, these were meager attempts at patching up the problems. The reality was that the problems were not process problems but mental model problems. Certainly, quality was an issue for many firms during the early 1990s, but it was just one of the many complex problems that companies faced in that decade.

Numerous other ideas were proposed during the late 1980s and early 1990s. Jay Mendell in his 1985 book *Nonextrapolative Methods in Business Forecasting* (John Wiley and Sons, New York) suggested that linear planning models could be problematic at best. Gary Hamel and C.K. Prahalad, while hanging onto the concept of "core competencies," began to suggest that changes in complexity and rates of change of necessity meant a rethinking of the organization's strategy.[6] In response to the apparent failure of the competency-based approach to strategy, Henry Mintzberg penned *The Rise and Fall of Strategic Management* in 1994.[7] Mintzberg suggested that the field of strategy at that time was failing companies (which it was, in general) and that rather than attempting to think about strategy from a futuristic standpoint, organizations should simply allow strategy to emerge. Mintzberg's approach appears to have been based upon the concept of "bounded rationality." See Chapter 6 for a more complete discussion of that topic.

A number of theorists began suggesting that nonlinear tools would be more appropriate for understanding and dealing with complexity. Jay Mendell, Arie P. de Geus (see "Planning as learning" in the *Harvard Business Review*, July-August 1988), and Peter Swartz[8] advanced the idea that it was possible to deal with complex futures by using scenarios. In a number of situations, scenarios proved extremely helpful to corporate executives.

Around the same time, Peter Senge's well-received work *The Fifth Discipline* was introduced (1990). What Senge did extremely well was to move the complexity metaphor from the realm of natural science into the realm of business. He suggested that business environments often involved what he called "dynamic complexity." In such environments, he stated, linear planning methodologies simply will not work.[9]

Perhaps the most important contribution made by Senge was his popularization of the concept of "systems thinking." Rather than accepting Mintzberg's somewhat defeatist approach in looking at future complex environments, Senge suggested that it was possible to gain a reasonable understanding of complex environments. In contrast to those who suggested that complexity creates a situation in which the observer cannot understand the environment, Senge suggested that it was possible for the observer to make reasonable inferences about a complex environment.

He defines systems thinking as follows:

1 Seeing interrelationships rather than linear cause-effect chains.
2 Seeing processes of change rather than snapshots.[10]

In principle, Senge proposed that the human mind, as a complex system, has the ability to intuitively consider complex situations and further to make reasonable inferences from that information.

In recent years, the emergence of complexity literature from the more academically focused community has become more prolific. In my opinion, one of the leading academicians is Michael Lissack. For those who are interested in accessing some of the latest complexity thinking from academic circles, Lissack's 1997 presentation in Warsaw to the SCOS may be found on the Web at http://lissack.com/writings/warsaw1.htm.

Generally, almost all of the management-related books published between 1990 and 2001 deal directly or indirectly with complexity and chaos. In *Built to Last*, for example, Jim Collins and Jerry Porras suggest that some companies possess a "visionary" quality (or qualities) that allows them to prosper over many decades.[11] At the heart of their argument is the idea that those companies that do extremely well in the long term have visionary qualities that drive the adaptation of the firm through shifts in the environment.

In *Control Your Destiny or Someone Else Will*, Noel Tichy and Stratford Sherman make an excellent case for purposeful, directive, creative leadership as a way of dealing with complexity and frame-breaking change. In telling the story of Jack Welch and GE they discuss the dichotomy that organizations must learn to relate to when dealing with complex environments. The 1980s and 1990s produced a continuum of frame-breaking change. Rather than being a poster boy for proponents of self-organization, Jack Welch established highly structured approaches for dealing with environmental dynamics. Part of that structure involved human capital and knowledge. Welch insisted that people be a part of the solution and that they be willing to continually challenge the status quo in favor of a more profitable future.[12]

Richard D'Aveni's 1994 book *Hypercompetition* marked a real turning point in strategy and complexity thinking. What D'Aveni realized was that the world of the 1990s involved a higher level of complexity and greater rate of environmental change than had previously been observed. Thus, he proposed that the world had moved from a linear one (suited for equilibrium-based, simplistic approaches) to a world more characterized by uncertainty and complexity. One comment he made in the book reveals just how drastic his break with traditional management thinking really was:

> "My goal is to provide managers with a better understanding of the process of competitive strategic maneuvering and to help them make better strategic decisions in a world of dynamic motion where no action or advantage can be sustained for long. In doing so, I point out weaknesses in many of the traditional 'myths' that underlie strategies used in today's America. Strategic concepts such as fit, sustainable advantage, barriers to entry, long-range planning, the use of financial goals to control strategy implementation, and SWOT analysis all fall apart when the dynamics of competition are considered."[13]

The most recent work to focus on complexity is Shona Brown and Kathleen Eisenhardt's *Competing on the Edge*, which has received widespread acceptance. The authors see the company as a succession of competencies – they suggest the environment is one of changing pace and changing complexity, and conclude that the firm must involve itself in a harmonious "dance" of changing competencies.

One of the ideas for which they make an extremely good case is the need for managers to balance the past and the future. They suggest that even in dynamic, complex environments, there may be some historic products that will have value in the future. Thus, it is important for managers to avoid the trap of focusing on historic, product-related competencies, but at the same time they must be smart enough to recognize existing products that may have future potential.[14]

THE PAST, PRESENT, AND FUTURE OF COMPLEXITY THEORY

I began this chapter with a discussion of the complexity of the subject itself. What I have tried to do is provide some insight into the many diverse ways that complexity theory has evolved and, more importantly, how the reality of complexity has affected just about every area of business. From basic management theory to change management, to strategy, much of the work over the past 20 years has either explicitly or implicitly addressed complexity-related issues.

While a number of the assumptions that underlie a lot of the current thinking around complexity theory, self-organization and the like lack valid support in science and reality, the field offers substantial value to the management theorist. There is research from a number of areas that suggests that managers' "mental models" have much to do with their ability to successfully lead organizations in complex environments. Thus, once some of the erroneous assumptions regarding complexity theory are discarded, there is an opportunity to effectively utilize complexity-based thinking as a foundation for creating effective corporate strategy.

NOTES

1 http://www.acm.org/sigois/auto/Main.html.

2 Steiner, George A. (ed.) (1963) *Managerial Long-range Planning*, McGraw-Hill Company, New York, NY.

3 Ansoff, H. Igor (1963) *Corporate Strategy*, McGraw-Hill Company, New York, NY.

4 Ansoff, H. Igor (1990) *The New Corporate Strategy*, John Wiley and Sons, New York, NY.

5 Ansoff, H. Igor (1986) *Implanting Strategic Management*, Prentice-Hall International, London, UK.

6 Hamel, Gary and Prahalad, C.K. (1989) "Strategic intent", *Harvard Business Review*, May-June.

7 Mintzberg, Henry (1994) *The Rise and Fall of Strategic Management*, The Free Press, New York, NY.

8 Swartz, Peter (1991) *The Art of the Long View*, Currency Publishing, New York, NY.

9 Senge, Peter (1990) *The Fifth Discipline*, Doubleday-Currency, New York, NY.

10 Senge, Peter, *op. cit*, p. 73.

11 Collins, James C. and Porras, Jerry I. (1994) *Built to Last*, Harper-Business, New York, NY.

12 Tichy, Noel M. and Sherman, Stratford (1993) *Control Your Destiny or Someone Else Will*, HarperBusiness, New York, NY.

13 D'Aveni, Richard A. (1994) *Hypercompetition*, p. xiv, The Free Press, New York, NY.

14 Brown, Shona L. and Eisenhardt, Kathleen M. (1998) *Competing on the Edge*, The Harvard Business School Press, Boston, MA.

The E-Dimension:
Complexity

This chapter looks at the impact of technological change, the ten forces model, and complexity.

Complexity is reality in the wired world. The emergence of the Internet in the early 1990s marked a point in time from which the world would never be the same again. It marked a time when news was no longer the domain of news organizations but of people around the world who could communicate with each other in seconds.

In my attempt to discover the role of technology (and especially the role of the Internet, although it is nearly impossible to separate communications media now) as it relates to complexity, I found an interesting relationship between the two. In my book *Thriving in E-Chaos* (2001, Prima Publishers, Roseville, CA), I present a graphic that portrays the interaction between the two forces that primarily drive environmental "rate of change" and the eight forces that I believe primarily drive complexity. What I discovered was that while technology forces may have a serious impact on environmental complexity, they can have an extreme impact on the environmental rate of change.

Why is this important? While Fig. 4.1 infers complexity and environmental rates of change operating at similar levels, that is not necessarily true in reality. Moderate levels of complexity may not be too difficult to deal with if the rate of change in the environment is slow. However, if technological change (such as the Internet) is introduced into the equation, the acceleration of change in the environment may make even moderate levels of complexity near impossible to deal with.

A good example of the problem was the "I love you" virus, which was introduced to the Internet system by an individual in England around six o'clock in the morning. By noon in New York, many companies were scrambling to try to deal with the virus which had the potential to seriously disrupt their computer operations.

A cycle of change (or as some call it "frame-breaking change") is a sequence of events that occur in an environment that change the "rules of the game." In complex, dynamic systems (such as the global environment), these events can be at a manageable pace. However, the introduction of high-speed change which is the result of technology-driven events may precipitate extremely rapid alterations in the rules of the game.

This is where the field of complexity becomes extremely important. Complexity thinking in the management arena is an attempt to create mental models that allow an organization to dynamically adapt to

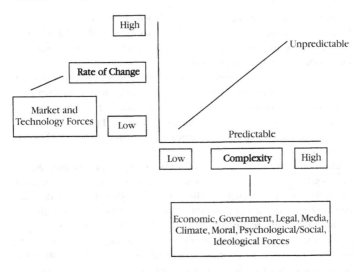

Fig. 4.1 The ten forces model. (From *Thriving in E-Chaos*, James D. Underwood, used with permission.)

environmental changes that subsequently alter the rules of the game. That is, complexity thinking becomes a critical tool in developing solutions to complex changes in the rules of the game. Technology simply adds speed to the complexity mix.

2001: THE NEXT SHIFT IN THE RULES OF THE GAME

In 2001, many technology manufacturers felt like they had a party and no one came. The hype over the future of technology in the late 1990s had led to massive overpricing of technology-related stocks on the US stock market. In fact, many people became enamored with the technological possibilities that were emerging without considering whether or not buyers would be willing to pay the price to obtain those technologies.

The much-touted 3G (third-generation) wireless network that would supposedly deliver broadcast-quality video streaming to a cell phone began to encounter numerous delays. Providers started to realize that the costs to bring up the network were so massive that the ultimate cost of service to the consumer might substantially exceed what they were willing to pay for such a service.

In the confusion, a couple of outcomes seemed to become predictable. The first was that the new 3G networks would probably be deployed on a limited basis. Further, the target for those services would initially be commercial clients instead of the average citizen. That would mean that 20 or so major markets in the US would be the initial target.

The other outcome is expected to be more widely adopted and to have significantly higher diffusion rates into the general population. I call this the emergence of the FID, or "fully integrated device." The FID will use a combination of devices plus a combination of technologies. The technologies involved will be DSPs (digital signal processors – devices capable of transforming analog signals into digital signals, such as voicemail or faxes) and softswitches (which will enable an individual user to "direct" all their personal electronic devices, such as office phone, office fax, office e-mail, home e-mail, home voicemail, home fax, and paging, to their FID).

The FID will be a converged device that includes computing, wireless phone, Internet (two-way), and the usual PDA (personal digital assistant) capabilities. More than likely, it will in fact be two separate devices, a cell phone and a PDA. It will be possible to link the devices so that the user has the ability not only to receive IP-based (Internet protocol) messaging from any other personal device (around the world) but also to respond using their FID.

Those who are able to get a 3G-based FID will be pleasantly surprised. One option with such a device will be phone-to-phone (or FID-to-FID) broadcast-quality video conferencing. That means that two people with 3G-based FIDs could have a real-time, face-to-face conversation from different parts of the country. Such devices could also make television programming available to the user.

The point of all this is simple, yet quite powerful. The disappointment of the early 2000s could become the next e-explosion of the century. The integration of devices, along with the new wireless networks (and a lot of the new light-spectrum technologies were not even put into the picture), could expand rapidly. One thing to remember is that many of the benefits related to the FID do not require 3G networks.

If, in fact, the FID emerges as I have pictured it, the implications for business and personal communications could be changed for ever. Not only would the complexity of the environment increase drastically, but the rate of change would accelerate significantly. That is a small picture of the possible e-dimension of the future complexity of the global environment. There is more.

THE NEXT THREAT

Many involved with corporate security believe that the next threat from global terrorism will not be in the form of random physical violence. Rather, they feel that cyber-terrorists from foreign powers will target selected electronic portals in a given country. Among the targets will be power-generation and distribution networks, as well as the telecommunications infrastructure. The result of such terrorism could be the virtual cessation of business in that country while the problems are resolved.

While the integration of FIDs could be a boon to global commerce even though it could enhance the level of complexity and chaos of the environment, the same is not true about e-terrorism. With e-terrorism, a few people in a remote part of the world could disrupt entire economies. This type of disruption would reveal the unbelievable levels of linkage and complexity that exist in the global community. Would it be possible to get food? What about a prescription? Would our telephones even work? The level of complexity in such a scenario is massive. (There are organizations that are quietly working on this problem, incidentally.) Some companies seem to be much more adept at preparing for the new economy. While it is possible to be on the bleeding edge of adopting new technologies (too early), one company, Fidelity Investments, seems to have the ability to appropriately stay ahead of most of its competitors without finding itself in trouble.

As Figure 4.1 shows, technology forces have a great deal to do with the speed of environmental change. That means that the impact of complexity is increased with the onset of accelerated environmental change. What used to take weeks or even months to impact an organization can now hit a company in a matter of minutes.

E-COMPLEXITY AT FIDELITY INVESTMENTS

In May 2001 I was given a tour of a new regional office of Fidelity Investments. Fidelity is a recognized leader in the mutual fund market. A privately held company, it has managed to balance excellent portfolio positioning with a leading-edge technology strategy. Fidelity's senior management have adopted a two-pronged approach for dealing with the complexities of the new e-dimension of the environment. First, their internal systems are second to none. Second, their technology philosophy is clearly that of being a consistent first mover.

One of the first places I was taken was the technology area. The best word to describe Fidelity's technology approach might be "global redundancy." Each technology process is continually challenged. Each one not only has redundancy, but there are alternative systems that back up primary systems. Behind the redundancy in local systems, there is still more redundancy in Fidelity's global area network (GAN). To the Fidelity customer, this means one thing: dependability.

Fidelity's system is so comprehensive that a customer could be working on their account online while a system goes down and the customer would never know it had occurred. In fact, the system is so good that the back-up system could also go down and the customer would never know that their processing had been automatically transferred to another part of the globe.

Fidelity's attitude carries over to the product development area. One would think that an investment firm would expect to use technology for the purpose of gathering information from around the world, but Fidelity's interest in technology goes far beyond such a limited view of the future of technology.

Behind the scenes at Fidelity there are people continually investigating the possibilities of the future of technology. Most importantly, they are looking at the numerous ways that their customers might use to access their critical account information in the future. For example, if a customer traveling in Europe or Asia needed to modify their holdings, how could they use existing or emerging applications to achieve that securely? Those are the kinds of questions that they ask continually at Fidelity.

Obviously, Fidelity Investments approaches the job with two ideas in mind: to ensure the security of its customers, and to use technology to anticipate customer needs. Not bad objectives for a firm that wants to maintain its leadership position in a highly complex and competitive field.

NOTE

1 Underwood, James (2001) *Thriving in E-Chaos*, Prima Publishers, Roseville, CA.

The Global Dimension

The global aspects of complexity theory are discussed in this chapter. Managers need to be aware of how events around the world can impact every aspect of their business.

If one is going to think about complexity, it is difficult, if not impossible, to think about it without taking a global perspective. In fact, in preparing to do almost any research, it is important to develop a "global model" of the area under study. Global modeling involves a detailed study of the numerous variables that may impact an issue, or dependent variable.

For example, suppose that a researcher wants to understand which variables (or forces) have an impact on corporate sales. Consider the variables that need to be grasped in order to develop a general understanding of this issue:

» the economy (international, national, regional);
» competitor activities (sales aggressiveness, advertising, pricing, etc.);
» the company's sales aggressiveness;
» the company's pricing strategy;
» value chain and distribution issues;
» the weather;
» legal issues;
» societal issues;
» the company's advertising;
» the company's public relations activities;
» product quality;
» product service quality;
» warranty issues; and
» the company's customer service (level).

This is a short list of the variables that may have a direct impact on a company's sales. Even this simple list is extremely complex. Reality is even more complex.

LEARNING TO THINK GLOBALLY

In June 1991, a seemingly insignificant event occurred in the Philippines. A volcano named Mt. Pinatubo erupted. Aside from the news reports about the ash that settled on a nearby US military installation, not much else was said about the event. Yet consider the impact.

The eruption was the third largest to occur in the twentieth century. It produced the greatest volume of sulfur dioxide ever produced by a volcanic eruption. The gas reached the stratosphere and circled the globe in three weeks.[1] Further, it is estimated that the global temperature decreased by 0.5 degrees Celsius. That year, the farmers in the US reported cooler than normal temperatures. As a result, crop yields were unusually low. The decrease in agricultural revenues had an impact on the US economy, which in turn had an impact on the global economy.

Global complexity thinking

Managers need to think globally. In the 1990s, Boeing Aircraft's failure to consider the Japanese banking meltdown cost the company dearly. That, in spite of the fact that numerous experts (and authors) had been predicting the event for years. From a complexity standpoint, it was not a question of whether or not the meltdown was going to occur, it was just a matter of when.

From a practical standpoint, how do managers learn to think globally? A good place to start is the "ten forces" that were introduced in Chapter 4 (Fig. 5.1). Since these are the basic forces that drive both complexity and rate of change, a study of the potential interaction of these forces can be extremely beneficial to a firm's management team.

The ten forces assessment would normally begin with a study of the eight forces that normally drive complexity. Notice the importance of understanding not only domestic issues but also global issues in this assessment. With regard to the forces that normally drive the environmental rate of change, the firm's intelligence team should already have much of the information required to understand those issues.

COMPLEXITY TRAINING AT NORTEL NETWORKS

In the early 1990s, the training faculty at Nortel Networks Learning Institute was given the task of developing a training program for senior managers (those just below corporate officer) from around the world. In looking at the challenges those managers faced, the faculty realized that complexity issues had to be at the top of the list. The team developed a one-day training exercise that was designed to help the managers realize the importance of understanding the impact of complexity on their daily decision-making processes.

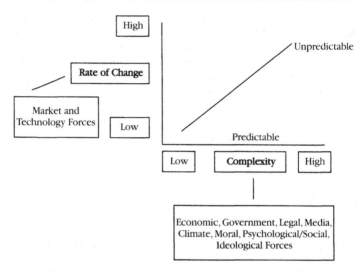

Fig. 5.1 The ten forces model. (From Thriving in E-Chaos by James D. Underwood, used with permission.)

One aspect of Nortel's complexity training required each attendee to draw a ''complexity map'' of all the stakeholders that he or she had to deal with on a continuous basis. In most cases, each of the managers had a minimum of 10-15 stakeholders that had an impact on their duties. In some cases, the numbers were more substantial. That simple exercise helped the managers to get a grasp on just how complex their jobs really were, and their complexity maps included only the internal personnel they had to deal with.

Assume for a minute that you are a senior executive for a computer manufacturer in the US in 2001. Consider just the global variables that you might have to include in your six-month strategic plan.

» Market forces - the dwindling economy of numerous global competitors may force them to drastically reduce prices, which could in turn substantially cut your firm's profits for the next six months.
» Market forces - the miscalculation of the global technology market has caused a near crash in the technology market. Many former

customers are going into insolvency, or drastically reducing purchasing.

» Economic forces – the new Japanese government is refusing to deal with many of the structural problems that are causing the country's economy to falter. There appears to be no hope for improvement in the near term.

» The global energy crisis continues to impact the cost of doing business around the world. Corporate profits are still diminishing, which in turn creates chaos in the global stock markets.

» Instability in a number of governments is creating substantial levels of uncertainty and unpredictability for future sales in those countries.

» Global e-terrorists may have the ability to shut down the economies of numerous countries, as well as corporate networks.

» Numerous ideological groups are threatening to disrupt commerce, travel, and tourism in a number of countries.

» Global terrorism is expected to increase.

» Unexpected flooding in numerous countries is having a devastating impact on those countries' economies.

» The outcome of the Microsoft antitrust litigation is still unknown.

Observe that this simple list is extremely limited in comparison with the number of variables (or forces) that the company really has to deal with. However, the list is helpful in leading to an understanding of just how important global complexity really is in effective corporate governance.

A PROCESS FOR DEALING WITH GLOBAL COMPLEXITY

The reality of global complexity and how global forces affect companies on every continent is clear. The real issue revolves around how a company should organize itself in order to deal with it. Many who hold a Darwinian view of complexity also suggest that incrementalism is the only way to deal with global complexity. That is, allow corporate strategy to emerge as issues emerge in the environment.

Such a view can be extremely risky at best. Consider the outcome for Shell Oil if Pierre Wack, the company's planner, had not anticipated the extreme conditions that led to the 1970s' oil crisis. Similar stories may be found throughout history. Were these incidents anomalies? Of course not. Research reveals that senior managers who can think in terms of complexity, change, and turbulence are much more effective than those who do not.

Further, complexity, and the difficulty of dealing with complex events, is often not the real problem. As Thomas Kuhn points out in *The Structure of Scientific Revolutions*, it is extremely difficult for people to change from one mental model (or paradigm) to another, even if their current paradigm is grossly mismatched with reality.[2]

Key strategies for dealing with global complexity

The reality of global complexity is unavoidable. The real challenge for managers is how they can learn to deal with it. The following ideas will go a long way toward addressing the problem of global complexity.

1 *Identify and use your people who naturally process complexity with ease.* (For more information see my article "Making the break: From competitive analysis to strategic intelligence," Competitive Intelligence Review, Vol. 6(1), 15–21, 1995, John Wiley and Sons.) Some people (2.5% of the population) are able to "see" the complex environment without paradigm biases. In some rare cases, those people can be found at the senior executive level of an organization. Executives who lead organizations well are those who are able to identify and use those employees who are gifted in processing complex information.

   Sir John Browne of British Petroleum is one senior executive who apparently has the ability to deal with complexity and further has the management skills to effectively use the complex thinking abilities of his people. In recognizing the increasing public concern with fossil-fuel pollution, BP now produces 10% of the world's solar technology, and markets that technology in 16 countries.[3]

2 *Develop a global intelligence organization.* Often, the business intelligence unit in companies does little more than database searches or buy "off-the-shelf" reports from industry vendors. That might account for the fact that it is often the intelligence organization that feels the budget-cutting knife first when the company encounters difficult times.

That should not be the case for a well-run intelligence organization. A well-conceived, well-run intelligence organization should be the information portal of the company. It should be a major contributor to the creation of profit potential.

3 *Use nonlinear strategic tools.* Linear, simplistic tools such as Porter's Five Forces and SWOT analysis are near useless in complex environments. In *Thriving in E-Chaos*,[4] I introduce two tools based on H. Igor Ansoff's work. The first is a complexity-based tool for predictive modeling called "environmental turbulence." The second is an organizational profiling technique that can be used to understand competitors' abilities as well as enabling corporate managers to understand the competitive strengths and weaknesses (not a simple SWOT analysis but a complex organizational assessment) of global competitors.

Further, two other nonlinear tools need to be understood and used. The first is scenarios, and the second is war gaming. There is research that suggests that both of these tools are better used as organizational learning tools (to reduce resistance to change), but I believe they can also be used to significantly enhance the organization's ability to effectively deal with global complexity. Ultimately, such learning would be translated into organizational strategy.

4 *Use technology to create a total learning organization.* More often than not, companies operate from the position that one mind (at the top of the organization) is more important and insightful than the 25,000 or so that the company has scattered around the world (the employees). Organizations that handle complexity well are those that do two things well. First, they understand that the level or amount of upward communication is directly proportional to the value placed on employees by those above them. Second, they understand that there must be a mechanism for gathering and processing information from all of the company's constituencies, especially its employees.

Technology solutions are the key in this case. The electronic media (such as the company's virtual private network) the company uses to run its daily business can easily be adapted for virtual learning. In some cases, I have seen firms simply create online information exchange and intelligence forums using Lotus Notes. In others, a more sophisticated program is created.

In either case, the information needs to go to the corporate intelligence team first. The second step is critical, but much more difficult to carry out. Once the data has been analyzed, it needs to go immediately to the senior executive team. It is imperative that it does not go up through a bureaucratic maze, since that virtually guarantees that dissonant information will be eliminated before it gets to the individuals who not only need to have that knowledge but have the power to initiate organizational transformation in response to the information.

5 *Develop a formal, "weak signal" issue management system.* In anticipating complex global dynamics, the most important information often does not come in the form of strong signals (the information developed from database mining or from information services). It comes from what some call "weak signals."

Weak signals are seemingly obscure and insignificant issues that surface occasionally. A good example of a weak signal was the indication (in the 1990s) that a company named Nokia had increased its research and development spending by a significant amount. That might have been important to a company such as Motorola, even though it controlled the market at the time.

A good issue management system assists the corporate intelligence team in categorizing the potential impact of the issue and then developing an appropriate strategy for dealing with it based on the potential impact of the issue.[5] Weak signal issue management is critical for organizations since complex dynamic systems, especially in a global context, rarely provide strong signals in a time context that will allow effective responses.

6 *War rooms and virtual war rooms.* War rooms simply serve as repositories for knowledge. It is preferable to have a physical site for a war room. That is, the presence of a "situation room" (or whatever you call it) that houses database access, competitor profiles, and key industry studies, and as such sends a clear message about the value that the organization places on the acquisition of intellectual capital and learning. From a practical standpoint, it is helpful if the war room can be made virtual with the ability to provide remote access as well as global video conferencing capabilities.

7 *Develop organizational practices to utilize systems thinking.* Rather than falling victim to many of the linear thinking approaches out there, make a concerted effort to apply systems thinking in every area of the company. Instead of teaching managers about systems thinking, conduct seminars to show them how they can learn to use systems thinking in their daily management lives.

CONCLUSION

Complex problems require complex solutions. Global complexity can silently impact an organization that is not prepared for it. It is abundantly clear that organizations can effectively deal with global complexity if their leadership supports the initiative and recognizes the bottom-line value of such efforts.

NOTES

1 http://volcano.cs.und.nodak.edu/vwdocs/Gases/pinatubo.html.
2 Kuhn, Thomas S. (1970) *The Structure of Scientific Revolutions*, The University of Chicago Press, Chicago Illinois.
3 http://www.www.ee/lisths/infoterra/1997/05/0061.html.
4 Underwood, James (2001) *Thriving in E-Chaos*, Prima Publishers, Roseville, CA.
5 Ansoff, H.I. and McDonnell, Edward (1990) *Implanting Strategic Management*, Prentice Hall, New York, NY.

The State of the Art

The state of the art of complexity theory is discussed in this chapter. Recent ideas are put forward, and there is an in-depth discussion of problems with self-organization (Darwinian hypothesis).

The debate that surrounds complexity is as diverse as the topic itself – by their very nature discussions about complexity increase in complexity to the point of confusion. There are numerous issues involved in these discussions, yet ironically, one of the major areas that needs to be discussed has not really been effectively covered up to this point.

This area involves the rate of environmental change. Certainly the complexity discussion has focused on using complexity theory from the natural sciences (as well as mathematics) as a metaphor for the business environment. Cybernetics, or the study of control processes in biological (and other) systems, has served the debate well (see W.R. Ashby's *Introduction to Cybernetics*). But there is more. In order to effectively move the complexity concept to the business arena, the issue of the rate of change needs to be included for the reason that, from a practical standpoint, as the level of complexity in an environment accelerates, so does the rate of change. "For a successful response to the environment, the complexity and the speed of the firm's response must match the complexity and speed of environmental challenges."[1]

It is reasonable to suggest that the forces that are the primary drivers for the rate of change also impact the level of complexity in the environment. This is best illustrated by my "ten forces model" (Fig. 6.1).[2] The idea is that eight of the ten forces are the primary drivers of the level of complexity in the environment and that two of the forces are the primary drivers of the rate of change in the environment.

From a business standpoint, the issue of complexity has mostly to do with decision making. Had it not been for the increasing levels of complexity and chaos between 1980 and 2000, it is suggested that little attention would have been paid to these topics. However, there was more and more evidence that resistance to change and the subsequent failure to lead organizational adaptation on the part of senior executives led to corporate problems. As a result, many management theorists began looking toward science for metaphors that would help them understand the complexity in business.

As early as 1957 Herbert Simon proposed that the complex nature of existence and the limited nature of the human mind to deal with such complexity meant that decisions must of necessity be made

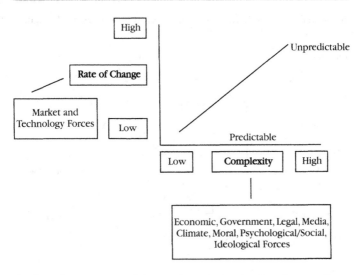

Fig. 6.1 The interaction of the ten forces in accelerating change and complexity. (From *Thriving in E-Chaos*, James D. Underwood, used with permission.)

with incomplete information or understanding. He called that problem "bounded rationality." Others, such as Peter Senge, suggested that complexity could be dealt with by using a concept called "systems thinking."[3] He suggested that the key is to seek to understand not the detailed complexity of a system but its dynamic complexity. He said systems thinking involved two key changes in mental models:

1 seeing interrelationships rather than linear cause effect chains; and
2 seeing processes of change rather than snapshots.[4]

The problems involved in thinking about or developing effective mental models concerning complex environments are best understood by taking a look at what is called "global modeling."[5] Assume your company is in the acorn business. A lot of things affect your industry. Some of those "things" are called independent variables. That is, they may or may not cause other variables called "dependent variables" to change. Let's consider your company, Acorn Industries, in the light of the ten forces model (Fig. 6.2).

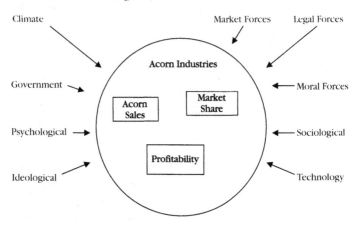

Fig. 6.2 The ten forces model.

This simplistic model of Acorn Industries reveals the challenges that corporate managers face in attempting to account for all of the variables that impact their sales, market share, and profitability. A simple change in the climate could have a serious impact on the company. So could a class action lawsuit, or new government regulations. The implications of just these simple variables are significant. Keep in mind that this is a simple model and is by no means reflective of the actual level of complexity that the management of Acorn must consider.

Now add to the mix critical changes in technology and market forces. Suddenly the speed of the external environment has discontinuously changed, and all the internal systems of Acorn Industries are designed for a much lower level of environmental speed (and probably a lower level of complexity).

EMERGENT OR PROACTIVE STRATEGY?

Some in the strategy business, such as Henry Mintzberg[6] and Ralph Stacey,[7] suggest that the overwhelming complexity of the environment (and the resulting "bounded rationality"[8] of human actors) means that proactive strategy is not possible. Thus, according to them, strategy must simply emerge. I have termed such "after the fact" thinking "incrementalism." That is, companies incrementally respond to events after they have occurred. This is important, especially in complex, chaotic environments. At the same time, by no means should emergent strategy be used exclusively – proactive strategy is not only necessary but reasonable. (Ralph Stacey, author of one of the leading books on complexity and strategy, once made the following statement to me: "Okay, I'll give you this much. If you find something that you can accurately predict in the future, use it. But such events will be few and far between.")

ECOLOGICAL MANAGEMENT AND DARWINIAN EVOLUTION

In 1998, I had the opportunity to attend a seminar featuring Peter Senge, the author of *The Fifth Discipline*. I had supported his concept of systems thinking for a long time and was excited about learning more. Around 2000 academics and corporate types attended the seminar. As I settled into my seat I was hoping to learn even more about systems thinking, especially about how organizations could effectively implement the concept. All went well for the first hour or so, then Senge began to articulate the philosophies that underlie his work. I had taken a course on modern theology at seminary and as a result had been exposed to the idea of imposing the Darwinian mental model on other disciplines. In religious circles, this idea of forcing an idea into theology is called "radical theology."

Much to my surprise, the rest of Senge's seminar focused on Darwinian evolution and how management systems are metaphorically similar to biological systems. Additionally, I discovered that much of what he was saying was clearly an adaptation of New Age philosophy. (One of the tenets of New Age philosophy is that "you are god." The inference is that causality is not rooted in the god of theism but rather in the "god in you." That is the idea behind the bumper stickers that read "visualize world peace." The logic behind the idea is that since you and I are god, if we visualize something, we can ultimately exercise causality in creating whatever we are visualizing.

Both Darwinian evolution and New Age philosophy are antithetical to a classic theistic world view. Since both require that the idea of an omnipotent, omniscient god be discounted to support their view, it is not unusual to find commonality in their supporters.)

Out of the Darwinian model of evolution comes ecological management. The hypothesis is that since nature is complex, dynamic, and evolves continually (and improves) autonomously, companies must (and should) do the same thing. Thus the primary role of corporate management becomes that of creating conditions under which organizational evolution will take place. This is generally referred to as "self-organization." In other words, the job of management is to get out of the way so that organizations can effectively evolve to a higher state, just like the evolution that takes place in nature.

Most theorists who deal in the area of complexity end up making the leap to the presupposition of a Darwinian evolutional mental model. Accordingly, most generally move to the next logical (some would say illogical) conclusion regarding self-organization of companies.

Back to the seminar. The afternoon session was an open forum in which the participants could ask any question they desired. Finally, my turn came to question Peter Senge: "Over the past eight years, I've been studying some of the most successful organizations in the world. What I don't see is self-organization. What I see is charismatic, change-oriented leaders who are obsessed with getting to the future first. Certainly, they understand the value of treating their people with excellence and empowerment, but at the same time, companies that are engaged in dynamic renewal seem to be those that are led by these purposeful people committed to dynamic renewal."

Senge's response was simple: "I can't say that I disagree with your observations. Is there another question?"

That transaction reveals the problem facing those who propose such self-organizing philosophies. The preponderance of the evidence simply does not support the view. But there is more.

A PROBLEM OF FOUNDATION

"I know that there is no evidence to support the theory of evolution, but I believe with all of my heart that some day we will find it." So said one of the world's leading evolutionists at the conclusion of a debate with one of the leading opponents of the view.

So, exactly what was he saying? He was recognizing the fact that evolution is more about faith than it is about fact. Consider the following.

» There are no transitional life forms in the fossil record. It would stand to reason that if there were such a thing as Darwinian evolution, along with all the other fossil records there would certainly be some transitional life forms. None other than Darwin himself recognized the dissonance between reality and his hypothesis:

> "Why is not every geological formation and every stratum full of such intermediate links [transitional life forms]? Geology assuredly does not reveal any such finely graduated organic chain; and this is the most obvious and serious objection which can be urged against the theory [of evolution]."[9]

» There is no evidence of one species becoming another. This is similar to the statement above, but points out an additional problem with the evolutionary hypothesis. If we see absolutely no evidence that one species will "evolve" into another, how can evolutionary theories have any credibility?

» In nature, mutations do not survive. In fact, mutants are usually destroyed by their own species.

» Science is revealing that vestigial organs have a function. A number of evolution's proponents have long argued that apparently "useless" organs in humans (such as the appendix) are proof that humans have evolved, and that the organs are no longer useful in the higher life form which is the result of evolution. Not so, the evidence is now revealing. The appendix, for example, serves as a "trash can" for the body.

Some years ago, a number of evolutionists stated that if they ever found evidence that humans and dinosaurs had lived at the same time, the Darwinian hypothesis would be questionable at best.

More than 20 years ago heavy rain caused a flood near the town of Glen Rose, Texas. As the waters receded, a man walking along a creek bed began seeing large tracks in the rock that the rushing waters had uncovered. Further investigation revealed that the tracks were those of a dinosaur. The detail of the tracks was so clear that the groove left by the dinosaur's tail was also clearly discernable. I had the opportunity to visit the site a few years later and found that the story was true. Even the claws of the dinosaur's foot were distinctly visible.

The dinosaur was not alone. As you follow its tracks up the creek bed, a second set of tracks joins those of the dinosaur. They are the tracks of a young boy (or girl). It is apparent that the child followed the dinosaur's tracks up the creek bed. Some fluke of nature apparently covered both the tracks at a later date. But the tracks remained in the mud and become solid rock over the centuries.

In 1998 the prestigious National Academy of Sciences (NSA) developed a book designed to address the rising criticism of evolution. *Teaching About Evolution and the Nature of Science* (1990, Doubleday Publishers, New York) was designed for distribution to teachers. Jonathan D. Sarfati, an accomplished scientist, decided to investigate the concepts put forward in the NSA book. In each case he found scientific evidence that contradicted each point. His research is presented in *Refuting Evolution* (Master Books, 1999) and more than 175,000 copies have been printed since the book was published.

So, what can be said about Darwinian evolution? As the renowned evolutionist in the debate suggested, the evidence supporting the hypothesis is nonexistent to this point. In fact, as John Sarfati points out in his book, there is an expanding body of evidence that disproves evolution. Does that mean it will never be discovered? No. But when the questionable nature of the entire hypothesis is considered, the reality at this point in time is that there is a lack of evidence to support it. This leads to an obvious question: If the evolutionary hypothesis has no proven validity, and in fact evidence is emerging that disproves it, why in the world would a rational person use the hypothesis as a basis for a management theory? The answer should be obvious: there is no good reason to do such a thing.

(Note: some suggest that a hypothesis is a proposed explanation of a set of facts. Once the hypothesis is tested, and the evidence accumulates to support it, the hypothesis may be classified as a theory.

Therefore, in applying this analogy to the evolution issue, it should not be classified as a theory, just a hypothesis.)

AUTOPOIESIS AND SELF-ORGANIZATION

The complexity paradox is alive and well in both science and management theory. One of the primary assumptions in most of these theories is self-causality.[10] Autopoietic theory holds to such ideas as self-creation, self-configuration, self-steering, etc. At the same time, while many in the scientific community suggest that creation is constantly exercising such self-causality (including the "big bang" that started it all), they further suggest that the world is continually evolving to a higher state. The first and second laws of thermodynamics reveal the opposite. Additionally, many of those same scientists suggest that pollution of the environment will result in certain highly predictable outcomes (not chaotic).

In the real world of business, we do not observe the supposedly natural evolution (upward) of organizations. In fact, we see just the opposite. Generally, organizations go through four distinct phases (see Fig. 6.3).

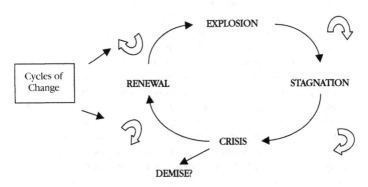

Fig. 6.3 The four-phase cycle of organizations. (From *Thriving in E-Chaos*, James Underwood, reproduced with permission.)

As a system, a company operates within a much larger system. As the ten forces model reveals, that external system is not only at some level of complexity but is also operating at some level of rate of change. Inherent in complexity theory is the idea that linearity is not reality. That is, the actual state of the system we call the world is continually changing in complexity as well as in the rate of environmental change. As a result, companies are continually in strategic balance or in strategic imbalance. A company that is in strategic balance is one that has mirrored the changes in environmental complexity and speed within its own system.

Companies left to "self organize" will generally deteriorate rather than positively evolve. A true open system (organization) is one that is the antithesis of a self-organizing company. The ability to operate as an open system is the result of continuous management of the organization as a system. That is, marketing, innovation, product portfolio, management, culture, intelligence (organizational learning/decision systems), strategy, plus other general areas of the firm, must be carefully choreographed on a continual basis.

The dichotomy is that the environment appears to be chaotic and certainly has varying degrees of complexity. That is why it is so important to understand the four-phase cycle. This cycle reveals the downward spiral that results when organizations become leaderless. It is important to understand that the organizations referred to still have managers when they go through the different phases. At the same time, in each phase the organization becomes more internally focused. At some point it becomes a closed system, or almost so.

The *explosion phase* is the point in time that follows an organizational discovery. It might be a new product or a new way of doing business. During the explosion phase, organizations are usually risk tolerant and accept individual failure as the price paid for entrepreneurial behavior. During this phase, a set of heuristics begins to emerge. It may first be observed in the emergence of more strict policies and procedures, but ultimately it is visible in the form of the organization's culture. It is important to remember that during this process there has been an external process. The external environment, while the company has been becoming more linear and structured, has gone through a cycle of change. During that time, the level of complexity and the rate of environmental change have often altered radically.

The company then enters the *stagnation phase*. Rather than focusing on reinvention (an open system behavior that is the result of organizational learning), the company's management often institutes a "get back to the basics" approach. Profit margins begin to shrink, and some of the competitors it has ignored are beginning to steal market share. During this phase the environment has undergone another cycle of change. At the same time, the company has engaged in the pursuit of the "flavor of the month" game. These "flavors" are often called total quality management (TQM), process re-engineering, growth strategies, value chain analysis, and so on. Since the firm has become a truly closed system, no one bothers to ask the simple question: "What is the problem and how can it be fixed?"

By the end of the stagnation phase, the environment has passed through two distinct cycles of change (and so the "rules of the game" have changed twice), and the firm is still trying to figure out why a TQM program was not the total solution for its problems. The corporate bureaucracy has become rigid and enormous, so the company now looks like an antique in a slow-motion film clip.

The *crisis phase* arrives without much fanfare. Downsizing has become the new corporate strategy for dealing with the earnings decline. In many cases, senior management becomes paralyzed. The loss of intellectual capital and knowledge (i.e. the firm's brightest and best people) is now almost complete. The product portfolio is generally focused on stage III (mature) or stage IV (decline) products (*Thriving in E-Chaos* (2001) James D. Underwood, Prima Publishers, Roseville, CA). The company's management is left with two choices: go bankrupt or engage in radical renewal. In almost every case, renewal is impossible to execute under existing management.

For those that survive the crisis phase and enter the *renewal phase*, a carefully conceived plan of action is necessary. The new senior executive must understand that urgency must be blended with empowerment. That direction must be seasoned with creativity and freedom. Rather than focusing on self-organization, carefully enforced rules of entrepreneurship and engagement must be instituted.

Here is where many of the constructs of typical complexity theories fall apart. First, it is important to remember that the primary presupposition that underlies the thinking of many that work in the field is Darwinian evolution. As we have discussed, recent work has demonstrated that evolution is flawed from a scientific standpoint, and certainly should not be used as a metaphor for complexity-based thinking. Second, self-organization in the business arena appears to be similarly flawed. Those who think they see such self-causing relationships are simply imposing a presupposition rather than recognizing a business reality.

At the same time, this does not mean that complexity theory is not extremely helpful as a metaphor for business leaders. The reality of the business environment is that it is (and will continue to be) complex and dynamic. In fact, when the Darwinian presupposition is removed from the complexity mental model, managing in complex dynamic environments becomes much more reasonable. The solution? Complex adaptive systems.

Notice that I have replaced the idea of *complex adaptive systems* to describe the environment with the idea of *complex dynamic systems*. External systems simply exist. Further, rather than being quite so adaptive (as some hypothesize), it is better to think of them as dynamic (different levels of complexity and speed of change at different points in time). Further, it is possible to understand many aspects of these complex systems, even though they appear to be chaotic, and are nonlinear in nature. This does not mean that specific outcomes can be predicted, but at the same time the nature of outcomes can often be quite accurately predicted. In principle, this is the argument advanced by the systems thinker. It is possible to consider complex futures and make reliable inferences. (Notice that I moved the typical idea behind systems thinking from an historic/present paradigm to a future paradigm.)

H. Igor Ansoff developed one of the most insightful advances in the area of cybernetics and systems thinking in the 1980s. He hypothesized that it was possible to develop a metaphor that would accurately represent environmental complexity and rate of change. He called this metaphor "environmental turbulence."[11]

THE ANSOFF TURBULENCE INDEX

Ansoff believed that the level of complexity and rate of environmental change in the environment was generally determined by different factors that make up the marketing and the innovation environment. He further believed that it was possible to effectively predict the levels of each of these factors in the future. When combined, the two broad areas of the future market became what he called "environmental turbulence" (Table 6.1).

Ansoff developed a number of approaches for studying the future and determining which view of the future was most accurate. His approach includes internal managers' views of the future, perceptions revealed in literature, and industry experts as determined through the use of a Delphi Panel approach. (Delphi Panels were developed at Rand Corporation and involve the use of six experts in predicting future events or states. The approach has proven quite reliable.) In practice, this approach has proven extremely powerful.

By studying the future environment in this fashion, it is possible to take each "slice" of the future and synthesize it into a broader model of marketing or innovation turbulence. Once that is done, the two are synthesized into one final index on a scale of 1 through 5. As a result the index, as a metaphor representing the rate of change or level of complexity in the environment, assists the manager in understanding the reality of the future. A level 1 environment, for example, is predictable, simple, and slow-changing. A level 3 environment will be fast, predictable, and competitive. A level 4.5 environment will involve overwhelming competition, high levels of uncertainty, and major changes in the value chain. How important is this?

Managers who proactively anticipate change are significantly more successful than those who reactively respond to change after the fact.[12] Additionally, organizations (leaders) that understand the level of turbulence perform significantly better than those that do not.[13] Another important fact is that external experts (outside of a company) have a much more accurate understanding of an industry's turbulence than a company's internal managers (thus validating the need for Delphi Panels in understanding environmental turbulence).[14] It is appropriate at this point to re-introduce a revised definition of complexity:

Table 6.1 The Ansoff turbulence index. Adapted from H. Igor Ansoff, with permission. Reprinted from *Thriving in E-Chaos* (Prima Publishers) with permission.

Future marketing turbulence

	1	2	3	4	5
Market behavior (competitors)			Competitive		Highly aggressive
Sales aggressiveness	Low		Moderate		Very high
Marketing aggressiveness (Advantage/PR)	Low				
Market strategy	Serve customers		Grow market		Expand share
Industry capacity vs. demand	Excess demand		Equilibrium		Capacity significantly exceeds demand

Future innovation turbulence

	1	2	3	4	5
Innovation behavior (competitors)			Competitive		Highly aggressive
Innovation aggressiveness	Low		Moderate		Extremely fast
Technological change	Slow				
Innovation strategy	Follower		Product improvement		Product innovation
Customer strategy	Meet needs		Stay close to customer		Anticipate unrealized needs
Product life cycles	Long		Moderate		Very short

"The nonlinear or unpredictable interaction of systems within the global system in which there are still elements of predictability. Further, the apparently random interaction between those systems may reveal certain understandable and ultimately predictable outcomes, at least as to the nature of the emerging system."

Two other important findings have come out of recent research. Managers who are successful in higher levels of turbulence understand how to create an organization (leadership, culture, structure, entrepreneurial behavior) that will perform well in that environment. At the same time, internally focused managers (a closed-system versus an open-system mentality) are much less successful than their environmentally knowledgeable counterparts.[15] Additionally, and perhaps critical to the discussion, managers who understand how to manage the firm (as a complex system) in relation to the environmental turbulence produce significantly higher profits than those who do not.

WHERE DO WE GO FROM HERE?

Just because the evolutionary hypothesis (especially as it applies as a metaphor for complexity thinking in business) has problems does not mean that complexity theory has no meaning for the business theorist. In fact, by recognizing the reality regarding evolution, the theorist is in a position to investigate more meaningful and research-supported approaches to using complexity theory as a foundation for driving organizational performance.

It is important to remember that managers who are able to effectively comprehend the complexity and rate of environmental change are those who are capable of leading more profitable organizations. Additionally, by understanding that the firm is a complex system, operating in a complex environment, managers are better able to develop appropriate organizations that will be in strategic balance.

In conclusion, complexity is reality. The global competitive environment is characterized by the complex interaction (complex dynamic systems) that does not lend itself to linear thinking. At the same time, the complex global system does involve aspects that are predictable. Further, as the systems thinker would suggest, it is possible to make reliable inferences about complex dynamic systems. That is the role of complexity thinking in the new global system.

NOTES

1 Ashby, W.R. (1956) *Introduction to Cybernetics*, John Wiley and Sons, New York, NY.

2 Underwood, James (2001) *Thriving in E-Chaos*, Prima Publishers, Roseville, CA.

3 Senge, Peter (1990) *The Fifth Discipline*, Doubleday, New York, NY.

4 Senge, Peter, *op. cit.*, p. 73.

5 Emory, C. William and Cooper, Donald R. (1991) *Business Research Methods*, Richard D. Irwin, Inc. Boston, MA.

6 Mintzberg, Henry (1994) *The Rise and Fall of Strategic Planning*, The Free Press, New York, NY.

7 Stacey, Ralph D. (1992) *Managing the Unknowable*, Jossey-Bass, Inc., San Francisco, CA.

8 In 1957, Herbert Simon suggested that the ability of the human mind to comprehend the complexity of a system was significantly limited when compared with the actual complexity of the system.

9 Darwin, C.R. (1972) *Origin of Species*, 6th edn, p. 42. John Murray, London.

10 Whitaker, Randall (2001), http://www.acm.org/sigois/auto/Main.html.

11 Ansoff, H.Igor and McDonnell, Edward (1990) *Implanting Strategic Management*, Prentice Hall, Hertfordshire, UK.

12 Friedank, Jan (1994) A dissertation: "Managing transformational change in German business firms," US International University, San Diego, CA.

13 Lewis, Alfred O. (1989) A dissertation: "Strategic posture and financial performance of the banking industry in California: a strategic study," US International University, San Diego, CA.

14 Lewis, Alfred O., *op. cit.*

15 Friedank, Jan, *op. cit.*

In Practice: Case Studies

A number of case studies of organizations are included in this chapter. The story of how one company trained its senior managers to handle complexity is discussed.

I will never forget a seminar I attended in 1998. The speaker was an internationally recognized author and consultant in the field of complexity. At one point during his presentation he made an interesting point. He said that a group of researchers had scoured the world and had found two companies that appeared to apply (his view of) complexity theory.

That leads us to two issues. First, it is difficult to find companies that actually apply the theories of complexity. (Executives rarely wake up and start their day with the intention of applying complexity theory to their job.) Second, the very nature of the theories surrounding complexity makes it extremely difficult to capture the practical aspects related to the topic.

As a researcher and a consultant I have been asked to do a number of projects that relate to complexity. In some cases in the 1990s I was asked to help different organizations to understand technology issues. I would like to begin with an overview of a company that handles complexity exceptionally well and then finish this chapter with some real-world illustrations. In Chapter 8, the term "complexity" will be used to refer to both the level of complexity of the environment itself and to the rate of environmental change.

COMPLEXITY: AN OPPORTUNITY TO PROSPER

Some might think that introducing the idea of complexity to a business situation would be a manager's worst nightmare. For many companies that is true. By our very nature as human beings, we like stability. We tend to think naturally in terms of stable environments. Further, even when confronted with complex dynamic environments (unstable environments), managers usually fail to change their mental models from linear to nonlinear. In reality, most people see little opportunity to enhance organizational profit in increasingly complex, turbulent environments. Most people, however, do not work at Microsoft Corporation, because at Microsoft carving profit out of chaos is viewed as the opportunity of the day.

LESSONS FROM THE TRENCHES AT MICROSOFT

Glen Agritelley joined Microsoft in 1988 as the head of an 11-state region that was managed out of Dallas, Texas. He was employee number 1530.

At the time, Glen had a staff of three people and sales of $2 million. By the time he left the company in 1997, his region had been cut to only four states but had revenues of $250 million and a staff of 160 people.

When asked about Microsoft's exceptional growth, Agritelley talks about things such as the culture and the attitudes at the company. In his opinion, Microsoft's ability to carve profit out of chaos is founded in the corporate machine developed and formed by founder and chairman Bill Gates. "When I was there," says Agritelley, "the values of Bill Gates and Steve Ballmer (now CEO) were passed down to every employee. You just understood that if you were going to work at Microsoft, certain things were expected of you. If you couldn't meet those expectations, you knew real quickly that you needed to find a different place to work."

According to Agritelley, there were three managerial values that were continually communicated:

1 Hire smart people.
2 Encourage risk taking.
3 Manage mediocrity out.

It is this ingenious blending of smart people, who are committed to excellence, who will continually engage in creativity and risk, that drives the firm on a daily basis. "The real story about Microsoft has never been written," says Agritelley. He goes on to talk about former employees who tell about the supposedly abrasive and challenging meetings with Gates and Ballmer. "You could prepare a 50-page proposal for them, and Gates would spend a few moments looking at your idea and go directly to the one or two weak areas of your proposal," he says. "What a lot of people did not understand was Gates' view of such meetings. A lot of people tried to dazzle him with their footwork, and that just did not work. What he wanted was for you to be right back in his face with facts. He expected you to have thought something through to the point that you could defend it. You have to understand the Microsoft culture is about continually reinventing the company. That means that every person is part of the intellectual capital of the firm. New ideas are everybody's job . . . it's just that Gates wanted everyone to approach new projects like the money going in was theirs, not the company's. He really expected you to know your stuff."

The exchanges that are often talked about are also further rooted in the Microsoft culture. Unethical behavior, for example, is never tolerated. That includes the company's behavior as a corporate citizen as well as a person's individual behavior. "You were never fired for telling the truth," says Agritelley. Further, he suggests, that commitment carries over to problems. The Microsoft executives believe that clear communication of what is broken is the best way to improve the company.

Living out of the box

According to Agritelley, the senior executive team at the time worked in unison to keep people from becoming complacent. "You were expected to stay 'out of the box'," says Agritelley. He credits the team of Bill Gates (now chairman), Steve Ballmer (now president and CEO), Jeff Raikes, Scott Oki (now retired), and Richard McIntosh (who has left Microsoft) with fostering that environment.

Agritelley goes on to explain that every manager was expected to have at least one customer-related project at all times. Regardless of their functional area, managers were expected to have a "hands-on" project to keep them involved in understanding customer issues. In a lot of cases, the managers were encouraged to take projects that were out of their general area of expertise so that, for instance, the product development manager would work directly on a customer-related issue.

Gates and Ballmer continually focused on what they called "customer needs." They believed that if a company was able to focus on just that area, it had to be successful. "That obsession has often been misunderstood as a desire on Microsoft's part to dominate the market," says Agritelley. "In reality, their goal was to dominate the customer's heart."

A lot of their attitude is apparently rooted in both executives being somewhat paranoid about change and competition. Agritelley suggests that Microsoft's market since the late 1980s has been characterized by extremely rapid market changes.

Both Gates' and Ballmer's understanding of the complex nature of the marketplace is revealed in the basic thrust of everything that the company does. According to Agritelley, their daily goal is to "disrupt the market with speed and product leadership." They also hold to the idea that "the competition of today is not the competition of tomorrow." That attitude has served Microsoft well. "IBM's OS2 could have put us out of business," says Agritelley. "The only way we survived that challenge was to provide a better product, faster, that more closely met the customer's needs."

There is another idea that underlies Microsoft's ability to deal well with complexity. It relates to the company's (leadership) mental model of how it will compete. Many of those familiar with corporate strategy will recognize the term "first mover." For some, the idea of being first to innovate, first to market, is not an attractive proposition. In fact, a lot of people call it being on the "bleeding edge versus the leading edge." Some strategists believe that being a fast follower is preferable to being a first mover. Many who hold to an emergent view of complexity would insist that this is the proper view. Not so with Microsoft. Consider the following quote.

"In any competition their [Microsoft's] goal is to change the rules of the game and to force the competitor to follow."

Microsoft is managed with a view to excelling in an uncertain environment. It's a "meritocracy." Those who lead well and create opportunity for the company are both recognized and rewarded for their achievements. Glen Agritelley tells of how he was selected as one of the company's "Manager of the Year" winners in 1991. With the award went a $10,000 Rolex watch. "They really appreciate people who help them get to the future first," he says.

Microsoft managers also have to rank all their direct reports each year. The top-ranking employees are given stock options. Title or rank is unimportant in the ranking, says Agritelley. The top 10% of employees could include an administrative manager or a mail clerk.

There is another reason that the company does well in complex environments. Despite appearances, Microsoft is not a single large company. It is a complex company. It is a network of small, entrepreneurial companies that have the freedom to identify and meet customer needs, just as if they were a stand-alone organization. In describing his job as head of a region for Microsoft, Glen Agritelley says he was given four basic philosophies on which to operate his district:

1 Conformity is not expected.
2 Run your district to maximize performance.
3 Maximize customer satisfaction.
4 Develop your people.

These four philosophies are extremely important – in analyzing companies that handle complexity well, these four ideas always seem to be emphasized. In talking about the four philosophies, Glen Agritelley goes on: "Those philosophies create a solutions-driven versus a problem-driven environment. Their attitude was 'tell me what you've done – never ask permission.' It makes every person feel more like an owner than an employee. That's real empowerment."

Another characteristic of companies that handle complexity well is their attitude toward mistakes. In a linear (mental model) organization, making mistakes indicates a deviance from control heuristics. At Microsoft, there is a different mentality about mistakes. The question of mistakes is not nearly as important as the question of how many mistakes you have made trying to make a positive difference for Microsoft's customer.

In summing up his experience at Microsoft, Agritelley says he walked away with four important behaviors for organizations.

1 *Take risk*. Organizations competing in complex environments are generally not dealing with a succession of predictable events. Just the opposite is true. As cycles of change drive the environment to create new "rules of the game," the firm must continually be engaged in creating and/or discovering the new rules. Compliance-based, linear thinking and behavior simply leaves the firm stuck in an old paradigm. Entrepreneurial risk taking challenges old paradigms and helps the firm deal effectively with complex dynamic environments (systems).
2 *Change the rules*. In turning Chrysler Corporation around, Lee Iacocca borrowed a saying: "Either lead, follow, or get out of the way." In complex environments, a company's leadership must determine whether or not they are going to be defenders (incrementally

respond to discontinuous events) or aggressors (proactively engage in changing the rules of the game). There is no middle ground.

3 *Run it (your area of responsibility) like it's your own company.* A number of years ago the term "intrapreneur" was coined to describe someone inside an organization who exhibits a high level of entrepreneurial behavior. Such behavior is a "critical success factor" for organizations competing in complex environments.

4 *Push-back is important.* In some companies, challenging a superior is viewed as insubordination (and some wonder why supposedly "excellent" companies get into trouble). At companies that handle complexity well, push-back is expected. At Microsoft and other companies that continue to thrive in complex times, every employee is expected to be willing to defend their position. (In reality, that's the only way a company can live "out of the box." If you have to fight with your manager about doing the right thing, your company is in real trouble.)

In looking at how those four behaviors played out at Microsoft, Glen Agritelley comments on how they were put into practice. He says Bill Gates had the attitude that "if you can't challenge me, you can't work for me." The result of that attitude, according to Agritelley, is that it makes ideas more important than egos or position. It also leads to openness within the company to share ideas in a more matrix-like, informal structure. At Microsoft, for example, different areas of the company periodically communicated new "best practices" that the division had developed. As a result, entrepreneurial creativity could be spread rapidly throughout the firm.

The complexity paradox is apparent at Microsoft Corporation. On one hand, there are fairly rigid and uncompromising standards related to creativity, risk taking, customer focus, and changing the rules of the game. On the other hand, it is apparently Microsoft's leaders' ability to sustain those practices that enable the firm to be an innovation leader on a global basis. Again, this is not a philosophy that is limited to Microsoft. It is apparent in most of the global companies that have demonstrated that they can continuously engage in the process of dynamic renewal. Putting it simply: reinvention is never an accident. Reinvention in complex environments is the result of a plan and a strategy that drives open systems behavior that results in continual organizational renewal.

KEYS TO DEALING WITH COMPLEXITY

Learning about complexity has some importance in understanding how to deal with complexity. At the same time, once a manager understands (develops a mental model that is complexity-based) that the business environment is a complex dynamic system, the real challenge is how to develop complexity-based strategies that allow the firm to mirror the complexity of the environment. H. Igor Ansoff's strategic success theorem may put it best:

"In order to maximize return on investment, the aggressiveness of the firm's strategies and the responsiveness of the firm's management capability must match the turbulence of the environment."[1]

The Ansoff turbulence index (using a scale of 1–5) metaphorically represents both the complexity of the competitive environment and the rate of change (Table 7.1). At level one, for example, change is quite slow, as is complexity. Level five is the antithesis of level one. You will find a simplistic view of the Ansoff turbulence scale in *Thriving in E-Chaos*.[2]

A number of data-gathering approaches are used to determine the level of each area being measured. In the case of the Ansoff model, the issue is the future, and not the present. The idea is to systematically develop an understanding of the future competitive environment as it relates to complexity and rate of change. Generally, the indexes developed out of future marketing turbulence and future innovation turbulence are averaged to create a future environmental turbulence index.

It is important to remember that turbulence is developed only for a competitive segment. That means that further analysis of the global environment is necessary. The ten forces model should be used as a starting point for such an analysis. In the end, the more complex the analytical process used for complex futures, the more reliable the inferences.

Table 7.1 The Ansoff turbulence index. Adapted from H. Igor Ansoff with permission.

Future marketing turbulence

	1	2	3	4	5
Market behavior (competitors)					
Sales aggressiveness	Low		Competitive		Highly aggressive
Marketing aggressiveness (Advantage/PR)	Low		Moderate		Very high
Market strategy	Serve customers		Grow market		Expand share
Industry capacity vs. demand	Excess demand		Equilibrium		Capacity significantly exceeds demand

Future innovation turbulence

	1	2	3	4	5
Innovation behavior (competitors)					
Innovation aggressiveness	Low		Competitive		Highly aggressive
Technological change	Slow		Moderate		Extremely fast
Innovation strategy	Follower		Product improvement		Product innovation
Customer strategy	Meet needs		Stay close to customer		Anticipate unrealized needs
Product life cycles	Long		Moderate		Very short

Once the future turbulence index is developed, the planner should have a fairly accurate understanding of the nature of the future environment. For example, value chain characteristics, competitor aggressiveness, and technological changes are just a few of the indicators that come out of such an analysis. Practical experience reveals that the turbulence analysis process also can indicate specific product changes. For example, in work I did for an electrical utility in the mid-1990s, a future turbulence study plus a ten forces analysis resulted in the following predictive analysis.

Findings

» Any attempt to apply lessons from other deregulated industries should be approached with caution. The inferences which can be applied are as follows.

1 *Pricing pressures* will probably impact the electric utility industry much in the same way as they have impacted other industries. As a result, electric utility firms should anticipate the continual slide of their stock prices.

2 Firms that paid a great deal of attention to *organizational flexibility and aggressiveness* (first-mover advantage) have tended to do significantly better than firms that did not.

3 Firms that have been willing to *diversify outside of core business areas* (discontinuous-unrelated and discontinuous-related innovation) have generally experienced revenue and profit growth.

» An approach of seeking "*value added*" service and product opportunities *could be quite damaging* if this strategy were viewed as anything other than a minor aspect of the firm's strategy.

» Electric utility firms that seek to emulate the apparent related-product diversification strategy, which has been successful in the telecommunications industry, must recognize that for the telecoms industry *the diversification strategy involved entirely new business areas*. Therefore, the successful electric utility firms will move toward unfamiliar high-growth business opportunities if they are to enjoy equal growth opportunities.

» Any assumptions related to the rate of deregulation could be very risky. The possibility of antitrust as well as legislative action suggests that *contingency plans for rapid deregulation* and reregulation need to be in place immediately.

One assessment developed out of the research proved quite interesting, especially considering the fact that the research was developed more than five years ago.

Strategic inferences which may be developed from the research

Summary: single-industry competitors will have a difficult time in the future electric utility market. There are strategic keys for future success that can be inferred from the research. First, organizations must become aggressive, market-oriented, flexible competitors in their core business areas (electric utilities). Second, they must be willing to break through historic thinking approaches and be willing to compete in new product areas.

Notice that the analysis does not predict industry events, yet it provides extremely powerful insights into the nature of the future environment. It would stand to reason that any company that engaged in discontinuous innovation (outside of historic competencies) would be more successful than those that did not. History has proven (as of 2001) that to be true.

At the same time, it is important to note how complexity is at the heart of the analysis. It might be reasonable to suggest that understanding the future level of complexity of the environment leads an organization to higher profit opportunity. Certainly that is true.

DEVELOPING A SYSTEMATIC PROCESS FOR DEALING WITH COMPLEXITY

There are numerous lessons to be learned from companies that handle complexity effectively. Further, a lot can be learned from studying processes for dealing with complexity. Fig. 7.1 provides a snapshot of a systematic process for dealing with complexity. It is always important to remember that the very nature of reality is that it is always more complex than any visual representation is able to convey. With that in mind, consider the key aspects of an effective process for dealing with complexity.

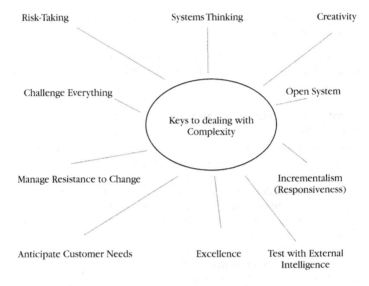

Fig. 7.1 A systematic process for dealing with complexity.

In looking at the keys for developing a system for dealing with complexity it immediately becomes obvious that there must be a blending of culture and practice. Each of these keys is clearly apparent at companies that handle complexity well. Risk taking is usually rewarded at companies that thrive in highly complex environments. An organization's ability to encourage risk taking and tolerate expected failures inherent with uncertain environments is key to maintaining the strategic aggressiveness of the company.

Systems thinking can be taught. In some cases, tools such as scenarios and war gaming can be used to encourage the process. It is also important to understand that in any organization there will be differences in people's ability to effectively apply systems thinking. Some, for instance, already think from a systems context, while in other cases it will be almost impossible to get an individual to a point where they can use it effectively.

Creativity is by definition a nonlinear activity. It involves either the creation of possibilities or the aggregation of a number of existing factors into an entirely new product or process. Creativity is the lifeblood of the future of the organization operating in complex environments.

Challenge everything is an attitude that sustains organizational reinvention. Companies do not fail because they failed to focus on their historic competencies. They fail because the external environment changed and the company did not. The "challenge everything" mentality accomplishes two critical organizational objectives:

1 It ensures that the historic products that are taken forward have the necessary profit potential.
2 It ensures that all external possibilities are included in the development of future strategies for the organization.

An open system mentality is reflected in everything an organization does. An open system is one that focuses on external instead of internal knowledge (such as politics). Open systems take their cues from the external complexity of the global system. An open systems mentality produces an organization that is highly adaptive.

The ability to manage resistance to change is important. Regardless of the culture and practices in a firm, it is always reasonable to expect resistance to change – it is human nature. Even when a company spends a great deal of time in developing appropriate ways of fostering complexity-based learning, managers in charge of implementation should plan for resistance.

Managers need to be extremely cautious about adopting some of the ideas about change that are presented in popular writings. There are three things on which a manager can focus to effectively drive organizational change.

1 Identify and segregate high-resistance personalities early in the process. At the same time, put the proactive change personalities on initial projects related to the transformation.
2 Avoid announcements. Instead, develop a modular implementation plan that moves the transformation into the organization in manageable "chunks."

3 Target 25% adoption. Research reveals that when a change is diffused into 25% or more of an organization, the change will normally flow on through the firm.[3]

Perhaps a fourth item should be added to the above. That is, in complex environments, transformation is continual. This idea may need further explanation. If the definition of management is changed from an equilibrium-based view to a complex dynamic systems view, it would be something like: the leading of organizational learning, transformation, and performance.[4] In a dynamic environment, organizational learning about the future should be a continuous process, as should transformation and performance. It is a "dance" in which the firm's leadership is simultaneously trying to maximize all three at all times. In the event that any one of the three does not occur, performance (present or future) will be diminished.

Incrementalism is a key behavior for the firm. As previously noted, incrementalism involves dealing with events after they have occurred. Some might refer to this process as "emergent strategy" (formulating responses after events). Basically, incrementalism is a poor substitute for good organizational strategy because companies must be both strategically proactive (future focused) and strategically reactive (address emergent issues). The bottom line is that companies in complex environments must be adept at both.

Companies must also be able to anticipate customer needs. In complex environments, "staying close to the customer" may be important, but it is no substitute for anticipating customer needs, an issue which involves understanding the complexities of the future environment. For example, in 1995, I was involved in a predictive modeling project for a major telecoms manufacturer. My research indicated that there would be a number of diverse technologies competing for my client's space. One reality was the convergence of computers and telephony applications. Further research revealed that the literature the client was reading (trade publications, etc.) indicated overwhelmingly that computer applications would be the application of the future. Based on the complex implications involved, one thing became clear. The customer needs of the future had to do with the conflicts between telephony and computer applications. Further, the customer was obviously going to need to be educated on how this convergence would impact them.

In this case, "staying close to the customer" would have been useless. The customer would have been of no use in defining this future problem. What the customer needed was education on how to deal with the numerous implications of this technological convergence. (It turns out that my assessment was correct – a number of problems began to occur with the integration of these systems.)

Excellence is a key commitment at organizations that do well in complex environments. As those at Microsoft or Southwest Airlines and others reveal, they all share a common commitment to excellence. Finally, these organizations test their mental models with external intelligence. As open systems, they focus on learning. In almost every case, these organizations use external intelligence as a comparison for their internal views.

There is one more issue: balance. History demonstrates that companies that commit to any one (or a few) of these keys can easily go bankrupt. It is the complex balancing of each of these capabilities that enables a firm to be in a state of continuous renewal. This may be the most important lesson that companies operating in highly complex environments need to learn.

A COMPLEX SYSTEM

It should be obvious by this point that complexity theory is both extremely important in organizational management in the new e-world and extremely difficult to simplify. Unlike process re-engineering or total quality management, it is almost impossible to synthesize complexity theory into a single idea or application.

Perhaps the most important point is the idea of "balance." Businesses operating in complex environments that focus on a simplistic set of competencies will fail. As a complex adaptive system, a firm must possess a complex set of attributes if it is to be able to have both proactive, future-based learning skills and high-speed, reactive learning skills. At the same time, it is important for the manager to remember that close studies of global organizations that deal effectively with complexity show that these organizations seem to share the same general characteristics. So, a good place to start in designing an organization that can maximize performance in complex environments is to focus on the ten "keys to dealing with complexity" discussed here.

NOTES

1 Ansoff, H. Igor (1990) *Introduction to Strategic Management* (working manuscript), San Diego, CA.

2 Underwood, James (2001) *Thriving in E-Chaos*, Prima Publishers, Roseville, CA.

3 Underwood, James (1995) "Making the break: from competitive intelligence to strategic intelligence," *Competitive Intelligence Review*, John Wiley and Sons, New York, NY.

4 Underwood, James (2001) *op. cit.*

Key Concepts and Thinkers

This chapter is about key concepts and thinkers in the field of complexity. The reader is introduced to a variety of concepts that help in defining the field. A number of key theorists are introduced.

With its roots in natural science and mathematics, the field of complexity can best be described as quite broad, and in many cases technical. On the other hand, business theorists have realized for a long time that an understanding of complexity is increasingly important for managers in this century.

The real issue in looking at complexity theory is understanding how to make it practical for the manager. The reader will often feel torn between a highly technical construct and the obvious need to be able to apply complexity theory to business application. While much has been written from a theoretical, technical standpoint, little can be found regarding the effective application of the theory, with the exception of works about emergence and self-organization.

In developing a compilation of the key terms, concepts (including their definitions), and key thinkers, I have attempted to cite those theorists who work extensively in the field of complexity, as well as those who seek to resolve issues of complexity in their work. In some cases, I have tried to summarize or restate a definition in order to make it clearer or more understandable. Additionally, I recommend the references cited as an excellent resource for those who would like to further investigate the field of complexity.

My purpose is singular. I hope to make as much of the technical material transparent while focusing on how managers can actually use complexity theory to maximize organizational learning and performance.

A GLOSSARY OF COMPLEXITY THEORY

Adaptive control – "An adaptive algorithm for control alters itself in response to information that it gets about the system that it tries to control."[1]

Ansoff, H. Igor – (Key thinker) H. Igor Ansoff, the "father of strategic management," was perhaps one of the first theorists to develop a complexity-based approach for strategic management. In citing the work in cybernetics by W.R. Ashby (a leading thinker and writer on the topic of cybernetics or the study of processes), Ansoff concluded that a manager's job had much more to do with dealing with the complexity and the rate of change of the environment than it did with focusing on historic competencies.

Ansoff developed a metaphor for the level of environmental complexity/change and called it "environmental turbulence." Further, he then began to develop organizational characteristics that he hypothesized would enable a firm to maximize return on investment (ROI) at each different level of complexity and rate of change.

Further, Ansoff believed that it was critical for an organization to be both highly responsive (which he called "management respon-siveness" - a form of incrementalism) and highly proactive about the future (which he called strategic aggressiveness). He developed a process for predicting the turbulence of the environment that enabled a manager to compare the present strategic profile of their organization with the future profile of the environment.[2]

After approximately 1000 studies, significant correlations between a firm's profitability and its match with environment have been deter-mined (known as Ansoff's "strategic success hypothesis"). Ansoff's hypothesis states: "In order to maximize return on investment, the aggressiveness of the firm's strategies and the responsiveness of the firm's management capabilities must match the turbulence of the environment" (Ansoff *et al.* (1993) "Empirical proof of a paradigmic theory of strategic success behaviors of environment serving organizations," *International Review of Strategic Manage-ment*). Generally, organizations that "match" using Ansoff's model will have return on investment of between 100% and 300% higher than those that do not match.[3] Based on those studies, it is suggested that Ansoff's "strategic success hypothesis" should now be called Ansoff's "strategic success theorem."

In using modified forms of Ansoff's turbulence model, I have been quite successful in accurately predicting environments. When combined with the entire Ansoff model, I have accurately predicted the future earnings of numerous companies. Further, I have accu-rately predicted the insolvency of companies. The point is that it is possible to apply complexity theory to the future. Additionally, in using the Ansoff turbulence model as a predictive tool in working with numerous international firms, including Fortune 500 compa-nies, the model has proven to be extremely accurate and reliable when used properly.

Aperiodic - The idea that "no variable describing the state of a system undergoes a regular repetition of values."[4]

Autopoiesis - "Maturana and Varela coined the term autopoiesis to characterize those systems which maintain their defining organization throughout a history of environmental perturbation and structural change and regenerate their components in the course of their operation."[5]

Bifurcation - "When a complex dynamical chaotic system becomes unstable, an attractor draws the stress, and the system splits."[6]

Bounded rationality - ". . . The capacity of the human mind for formulating and solving complex problems is small compared with the size of the problems that need to be solved for objectively rational behavior in the world."[7] (ref. Herbert Simon, 1957)

Brown, Shona L. and Eisenhardt, Kathleen M. - (Key thinkers) Two major contributors in moving complexity thinking from concept to application are Shona Brown and Kathleen Eisenhardt. Their excellent 1998 book *Competing on the Edge* is a "must read." The limiting aspects of the book are those that force the Darwinian metaphor into the management construct. Once past that problem, the book has a lot to say about maximizing both the present and the future. As with many others (D'Aveni, for example), they focus on a firm's ability to achieve organizational learning and to utilize that skill to create significant "first-mover" opportunities for itself. The book presents many solid approaches for driving creativity and risk-taking behaviors (critical for success in high-complexity, fast-changing environments).

Chaos - "Chaos refers in the world of dynamics to the generation of random, unpredictable behavior from a simple but nonlinear rule. The rule has no 'noise,' randomness, or probabilities built in. Instead, through the rule's repeated application, the long-term behavior becomes quite complicated. In this sense, the unpredictability "emerges" over time."[8]

Complex adaptive systems - An emerging view of the economic system that is being used as a metaphor for organizational systems. Complex adaptive systems are nonlinear in nature. The concept is based on three assumptions about systems: 1 they are open, and dynamic; 2 they are made up of interacting agents or systems;

and 3 they exhibit emergence or self-organization.[9] Also, the view of the organization that proposes that organizations operate in complex environments similar to nature. "Adaptive" refers to the assumption that nature evolves in the manner in which Charles Darwin suggested.

Complex dynamic systems - My view that the world is nonlinear and is made up of systems that may interact at various levels of complexity and at various levels of rates of change. This view differs from a "complex adaptive systems" view of existence in three ways. First, it does not presuppose a Darwinian hypothesis as the basis for viewing the whole system (and thus does not presuppose the validity of "self-organization" in either the whole system or in the firm). Second, it then defines the organization in terms of contingency. Third, while complexity is important, environmental "rate of change" is equally important in the understanding of how organizations must be managed. That is, the firm is a complex adaptive system that must "fit" the whole system, or the whole system will ultimately reject or regurgitate it.

Complexity theory - Complexity may be defined as the nonlinear or unpredictable interaction of systems within the global system in which there are still elements of predictability. In an interview with *CIO Enterprise Magazine*, Roger Lewin, a complexity theorist and author, said: "Complexity theory looks at systems in a way that are organic, nonlinear, and holistic." According to Lewin, the rules that guide the interaction between components of a complex system are: "1 managers should attend to relationships at all levels in their organizations; 2 small changes (in a system) can have large effects; and 3 interesting and unpredictable properties can be expected to emerge from a system."[10]

Constructs - "As used in research or social sciences, a construct is an image or idea specifically invented for a given research and/or theory-building purpose. We build constructs, which are more complex, by combining the simpler concepts, especially when the idea or image we intend to convey is not directly subject to observation."[11]

Content futurism - The study of a specific or limited area of knowledge related to the future, such as a specific technology.[12]

Cybernetics – "The theoretical study of control processes in electronic, mechanical, and biological systems, especially the mathematical analysis of the flow of information in such systems."[13]

D'Aveni, Richard A. – (Key thinker) "My goal is to provide managers with a better understanding of the process of competitive strategic maneuvering and to help them make better strategic decisions in a world of dynamic motion where no action or advantage can be sustained for long. In doing so, I point out many of the traditional 'myths' that underlie strategies used in today's America. Strategic concepts such as fit, sustainable advantage, barriers to entry, long-range planning . . . and SWOT analysis all fall apart when the dynamics of competition are considered," says D'Aveni in the introduction to his book *Hypercompetition*.[14]

D'Aveni, like others who wrote in the 1990s, discovered that the old linear ways of thinking were no longer serving companies well. In fact, he believed that those linear tools could be a formula for failure in the new nonlinear, competitive world. Generally, D'Aveni believes that a firm must be in a condition of continuous reconstruction. In principle, he suggests that rather than thinking in terms of historic competencies, the firm's management must think in terms of continuous dynamic reinvention. To some extent, he believes that the company that is able to create turbulence (uncertainty) for its competitors is the one that will be the long-term winner.

While a number of D'Aveni's ideas are quite commendable, his system falls somewhat short in the context of a complex whole system. At the same time, he has been one of the leaders in bringing the issues of environmental complexity and change to the forefront of corporate managers' awareness.

Detail complexity – An analysis or study of a complex microsystem. A good example of detail complexity would be the use of systems thinking in considering all the forces that might affect a company directly, without considering other forces. A detail complexity approach might also look only at a specific point in time.[15]

Determinism – "The belief that every action is the result of preceding actions . . . the idea that cause and effect rules govern science."[16]

Dynamic complexity – An analysis or study of the complex macro-system including the potential interactions of other systems as they might interact over time.[17]

Emergence – "Emergence is used to indicate the arising of patterns, structures, or properties that do not seem adequately explained by referring only to the system's pre-existing components and their interaction. Emergence becomes of increased importance as an explanatory construct when the following features characterize the system:

» when the organization of the system, i.e. its global order, appears to be more salient and of a different kind than the components alone;

» when the components can be replaced without an accompanying decommissioning of the whole system; and

» when the new global patterns or properties are radically novel with respect to existing components..."[18]

Equilibrium systems – A closed-system approach to economics that assumes and/or proposes linearity and predictability in the complex economic system. This concept was metaphorically applied to the modern ideas of competitive advantage, five forces, and most modern thinking in the field of management.[19]

Evolution – A process of change from a lower, simpler, or worse to a higher, more complex, better state (Webster's). The coming into being of a new and higher order of process (Laszlo). "The development of each species from different, usually simpler, ancestral forms."[20]

Five forces model – An approach developed by Michael Porter for assessing an organization's (micro) competitive environment. The five forces, according to Porter, include rivalry (among firms), threats of substitutes, threats from buyers, threats from sellers, and threats of new entrants.[21]

Game theory – "... A branch of mathematical analysis developed to study decision making in conflict situations. Such a situation exists when two or more decision makers who have different objectives act on the same system or share the same resources."[22]

Incrementalism – A term developed by James Underwood to describe a "responsiveness-only" attitude toward organizational strategy. That is, the idea of waiting until something happens before developing a strategy. This is tantamount to an "after the fact" approach to management. It is based on the views of some that conclude that high levels of complexity make future-based strategy impossible. The idea is closely tied to emergence.

Lissack, Michael R. – (Key thinker) In my opinion, Michael Lissack is the leading thinker in the field of complexity. He has a vast knowledge of economics, management, and securities, but his knowledge of the development of the field of complexity is second to none. I strongly recommend that anyone interested in the field of complexity visit his website at www.lissack.com.

Metaphor – "A figure of speech in which a term is transferred from the object it ordinarily designates to an object it may designate only by implicit comparison or analogy."[23]

Natural selection – (From Darwin's *Evolution*) "Selection is natural in the sense that there is no actor or purposive system making the selection."[24]

Noise – "All that is unpredictable about a problem."[25]

Open system – "A system with input, an entity that changes its behavior in response to conditions outside its boundaries."[26]

Paradigm – A mental model or construct of how a system or complex system is organized, including a definition of the "rules of the game."

Process futurism – The study of the whole system of the future. An attempt to consider the interrelationships of multiple complex systems and to understand and develop reliable inferences regarding probable outcomes.

Schwartz, Peter – (Key thinker) A number of the key thinkers featured have not been those who would be recognized as leaders in the field of complexity. In the case of Peter Schwartz, he does not claim expertise in the area. At the same time, he is a recognized expert in the area of scenarios. Scenarios are one of the tools that managers can use to deal with complexity.

Many people are familiar with the way that Shell Oil used scenarios to prepare for a highly uncertain future. While those who develop scenarios do not use the language of complexity, they certainly spend all their time dealing with it. Often, management tools such as scenarios and war gaming are less important as predictive tools than as learning tools. Certainly, scenarios and war gaming have been used to assess complex futures and accurately predict outcomes. Often, however, such exercises achieve a much more important objective: they foster systems thinking and organizational learning at the highest level of the organization. It makes sense. If it is possible to foster learning at the highest levels of the organization, where the power to implement resides, the resulting value of the knowledge is significantly enhanced.

In developing scenarios of future events, Schwartz recommends a detailed analysis of key factors that might influence the area under study. Once that is done, the analyst begins to develop three or four ways (or scenarios) that describe how those forces will interact with the issue under study. Ultimately, the researcher will evaluate each possible scenario and select one as the most probable.

By developing different scenarios, it is possible for the researcher to avoid (or at least attempt to avoid) personal bias. The construction of contradictory scenarios can have a substantial impact on the researcher's personal paradigm. (See also my article "Perspectives on war-gaming" in the *Competitive Intelligence Review*, 1998, John Wiley and Sons.)

Stacey, Ralph D. - (Key thinker) The author of *The Chaos Frontier*, *Dynamic Strategic Change*, and *Managing the Unknowable*, Ralph Stacey is widely known for his insightful approach for integrating complexity theory into management theory. As with most leading thinkers of the 1990–2001 period, Stacey rejects equilibrium theory (a linear approach to management mental models) as a basis for management theory.[27] He believes that the "old" linear mental models of managing will lead only to failure in complex dynamic environments. Instead, he suggests that strategy must be dynamic and emergent.

In *Managing the Unknowable*, Stacey lists seven steps that managers can take to effectively apply complexity theory to their development of organizational strategy.[28]

» Developing a new understanding of control.
» Designing appropriate uses of power.

» Establishing self-organizing learning teams.
» Developing multiple cultures.
» Taking risks.
» Improving group learning.
» Creating resource slack.

In principle, Stacey is suggesting seven behaviors that will enable an organization to continually challenge internal mental models. For example, he suggests that power in an equilibrium-based management approach would deal with compliance and control. In a nonlinear, dynamic environment, power would be needed to encourage creativity, risk taking, and therefore organizational learning. Through such learning, he suggests, comes an understanding of the complex, emerging environment. Then, once learning has occurred, organizational transformation can take place dynamically.

I once had a chance to meet some senior managers who had heard Ralph Stacey speak. They were quite impressed but had one concern. Emergence "only" is just not practical in most businesses. These managers were dealing with daily decisions that had to do with the future of their company years ahead. In my opinion, what most people fail to understand is that an organization needs both proactive (future-based strategy) and emergent (or incrementalism) strategy. It is possible to develop long-term strategy (3–5 years ahead) for environments of extremely high levels of uncertainty. That does not mean it is possible to predict the future. It simply means it is possible to make reasonable inferences about the future, and to understand the nature of the future.

Ralph Stacey does an excellent job of presenting an emergent, incrementalistic approach to organizational strategy and management. Many of the steps he recommends fit quite well with the behaviors of people like Jack Welch, who have used their power to foster high levels of creativity and risk taking. At the same time, it must be said that incrementalism, or emergence, is not the total solution. Other tools can be used to effectively create profit potential for an organization.

SWOT analysis - A concept first proposed by E.P. Learned, C.R. Christensen, K.R. Andrews, and W.D. Guth in 1965 (Business Policy: Text and Cases). SWOT (strengths, weaknesses, opportunities, threats) analysis is used to determine both an organization's internal strengths and weaknesses (and thus its unique competencies and competitive advantage) and its position in relation to the external competitive environment.

The ten forces model - A complex systems model that identifies the ten broad areas of systems that drive the macrosystem of a company. The ten forces are: economic, government, legal, media, climate, moral, psychological/social, ideological, market, and technological. Additionally, the model proposes that certain forces are the primary drivers of environmental rates of change, while others are the primary drivers of complexity.[29]

NOTES

1 http://www.santafe.edu/sfi/publications/Bulletins/bulletin-spr95/10control.html.

2 Ansoff, H. Igor and McDonnell, Edward (1990) *Implanting Strategic Management*, 2nd edn, Prentice Hall, New York, NY.

3 Ansoff, H. Igor *et al.* (1993) "Empirical proof of a paradigmic theory of strategic success behaviors of environment serving organizations," *International Review of Strategic Management*, John Wiley and Sons, New York, NY.

4 Mendelson, Jonathan and Blumenthal, Elana, http://www.mathjmendl.org/chaos/.

5 http:www.acm.org/sigois/auto/ATReview.html.

6 Mendelson, Jonathan and Blumenthal, Elana, http://www.math-jmendl.org/chaos/.

7 http://www.general.uwa.edu.au.u/kraepeln/bs/bs130/bounded.htm.

8 http://netra.exploratorum.edu/complexity/CompLexicon/chaos.html.

9 Beinhocker, Eric D. (1997) "Strategy at the edge of chaos," *McKinsey Quarterly* (1): 24-29.

10 Stantosus, Marge (1998) "Simple, yet complex," *CIO Enterprise Magazine*, April 15.

11 Emory, William C. and Cooper, Donald R. (1991) *Business Research Methods*, p. 71, 4th edn, Richard D. Irwin, Inc., New York, NY.

12 Barker, Joel A. (1992) *Future Edge*, William Morrow and Company, New York, NY.

13 The American Heritage Dictionary (1976) Houghton Mifflin Company, Boston, MA.

14 D'Aveni, Richard A. (1994) *Hypercompetition*, p. xiv, The Free Press, New York, NY.

15 Senge, Peter M. (1990) *The Fifth Discipline*, Currency Publishing, New York, NY.

16 Mendelson, Jonathan and Blumenthal, Elana, http://www.math-jmendl.org/chaos/.

17 Senge, Peter M., *op. cit.*

18 http://www.emergence.org/Emergence/Whyemergence.html.

19 Beinhocker, Eric D., op. cit.

20 http://pespmcl.vub.ac.be/ASC/Evolution.html.

21 Porter, Michael E. (1980) *Competitive Strategy*, The Free Press, New York, NY.

22 http://pespmcl.vub.ac.be/ASC/Game_theor.html.

23 The American Heritage Dictionary (1976) Houghton Mifflin Company, Boston, MA.

24 http://pespmcl.vub.ac.be/EVOLUT.html.

25 http://www.santafe.edu/sfi/publications/Bulletins/bulletin-spr95/10control.html.

26 http://pespmcl.vub.ac.be/ASC/OPEN_SYSTE.html.

27 Stacey, Ralph D. (1992) *Managing the Unknowable*, Jossey-Bass, San Francisco, CA.

28 Stacey, Ralph D., *op. cit.*, p. 188.

29 Underwood, James D. (2001) *Thriving in E-Chaos*, Prima Publishers, Roseville, CA.

Resources

This chapter provides an excellent overview of books and Websites that the reader can use to build a broad understanding of the field.

The field of complexity has exploded over the past ten years. People in diverse fields such as education, science, and business have become increasingly attracted to the study of complexity and as a result, resources have likewise exploded.

One thing the learner will discover is the similarities of complexity application in all fields. The presuppositions (the Darwinian hypothesis) are generally the same, as is the vocabulary. The following list of resources is by no means exhaustive. However, those who are engaged in discovering the breadth of resources available will find extensive links.

One important thing to note is that this chapter provides resources that differ from prevailing views. This inclusion offers the reader the unique opportunity to consider all sides of the argument involving the Darwinian hypothesis.

BOOKS

Competing on the Edge by Shona L. Brown and Kathleen M. Eisenhardt is an excellent example of the application of complexity theory to the management discipline. Some might suggest it is better described as a strategy book, and it has been used at a number of US universities as a textbook for graduate strategy courses. As mentioned earlier in this book, Brown and Eisenhardt apply the Darwinian metaphor in developing some areas of their approach. At the same time, they do an excellent job of presenting a number of proactive techniques for dealing with uncertainty and complexity. In some ways, there is a conflict between a futuristic mental model and an emergence-based mental model. Regardless, the book provides an excellent view of the application of traditional complexity theory.

The Chaos Frontier, Dynamic Strategic Change, and *Managing the Unknowable* (1992, Jossey-Bass, San Francisco, CA) by Ralph D. Stacey are exceptional writings. Stacey is extremely faithful to the emergence approach of strategy (incrementalism). At the same time he does an excellent job of providing the manager with ways of applying his approach in a practical manner.

Systems Thinking: Managing Chaos and Complexity by Jamshid Gharajedaghi (1999, Butterworth/Heinemann, Boston, MA) is an extremely good resource for those who want to understand how to apply complexity theory to the field of management. As we said earlier, in most instances there is a substantial chasm between theory and application in the complexity area. Regardless, Gharajedaghi provides a broad look at such applications.

Complexity by Mitchell Waldrop (1992, Touchstone, New York) is written with the reader in mind. Often, complexity articles and books are overrun with new language and concepts. Waldrop's personal, almost "folksy" approach patiently leads the reader through much of that maze. This is an excellent learning tool.

Strategic Renaissance by Evan M. Dudik (2000, Amacom, New York) is at the other end of the technical scale, but stands at the high end of the scale of applicability. One key approach in the book is Dudik's insistence that managers understand the future emerging environment (which he categorizes as deterministic, moderately variable, severely variable, or indeterminate) and then design strategy around the emerging environment. He also discusses what he calls the OCE (opportunity creation and exploration). In principle, Dudik suggests that as the environment becomes more uncertain, OCE activities become increasingly important to the growth and survival of the firm. This wonderful book provides excellent insight into managing in complex environments, without losing the reader in a maze of specialized terms. While Dudik does not attempt to write a complexity book, he provides excellent practical approaches for dealing with complex environments.

Refuting Evolution by Jonathan Sarfati was discussed earlier in this book. This excellent resource presents the opposing view of evolution and cites numerous highly credible scientists. The book was written in response to a National Science Institute publication for the purpose of refuting various propositions forwarded about evolution.

Phillip Johnson is the author of a number of books that question the Darwinian hypothesis. He wrote *Darwin on Trial; Darwinism: Science or Philosophy?; Reason in the Balance: The Case Against Naturalism in Science, Law, and Education*; and *Defeating Darwinism by Opening Minds*. For the scholar wishing to consider all aspects of the argument, these are well-written books.

SITES

Trying to present an exhaustive list of complexity and chaos Websites would result in a great deal of redundancy, since most complexity Websites provide extensive links to other complexity and chaos Websites. The following sites are those that serve as an excellent starting point for someone who wants to begin an extensive study of the topic.

As I have already pointed out, almost all theorists in the field presuppose the Darwinian metaphor as a basis for complexity. As a result few, if any, writers have questioned the foundational construct of the area. The three Websites that do question the hypothesis are supported by reputable professionals in their field.

The Santa Fe Institute (in Santa Fe, New Mexico) is a leader in the field of complexity. The institute has a full-time staff, plus faculty, and periodically brings in outside researchers to conduct additional research in the field. Additionally, the institute's training, which is offered to outside clients, is an excellent resource for those in science as well as business. The Website is www.santafe.edu.

An exciting resource for the field of complexity can be found at www.brint.com. This is an extremely well-developed and well-maintained site which offers a broad information base for the learner. Anyone interested in conducting research on complexity should make this site one of their first stops.

Earlier in this book, we discussed Michael Lissack at length. In my opinion, he must be viewed as one of the leading thinkers in this field. Therefore, his Website, www.lissack.com, is a "must" for anyone who is serious about learning in this field.

The Center for Complex Systems at www.cs.brandeis.edu/~brendy/ is another exceptionally strong Website. Brendan Kitts has developed a good site that offers access to a number of resources, including some excellent papers on the topic.

Fast Company Magazine features the more practical aspects of complexity theory. Its iconoclastic approach to featuring frame-breaking approaches, plus stories on complexity, can be quite helpful to the business reader. Fast Company's Website can be accessed at www.fastcompany.com.

A really excellent resource can be found at www.calresco.org/sos/ sosfaq.htm. The site features a number of frequently asked questions about self-organizing systems. It offers a comprehensive look at key issues and is a great vocabulary resource.

For those interested in depth, Randall Whitaker's Website, at www.acm.org/sigois/auto/Main.html, is quite good. As with most other complexity-oriented sites, it offers a lot of great links.

The resource that has perhaps the most complete depth and breadth in coverage of the topic is the *Complexity* (journal) Website at www.journals.wiley.com/complexity/. The site also provides information about past journal articles. This is an excellent resource, as is the journal itself.

The University of Colorado at Denver may be found at www.carbon.cudenver.edu. This site provides a lot of information on cybernetics, as well as an extensive set of links to other complexity Websites. The Institute for the Study of Coherence and Emergence also has an excellent Website. It can be accessed at www.emergence.org. Or visit the Society for Chaos Theory in Psychology and Life Sciences at www.societyforchaostheory.org.

A comprehensive listing of complexity Websites is available at www.udel.edu/aeracc/sites.html. This is the Chaos and Complexity Theory Web site.

LEARNING TO CREATE

A few years ago, Dr Toni McNutt of Synapse Decisions recognized the need to train leaders to do business in complex environments. She was most interested in helping them learn about the development of novel ideas for the purpose of helping managers understand the role of creativity in problem solving. There are just a few companies in the US that work in this area, and the approach developed by Dr McNutt and her team is quite powerful.

There are many definitions of creativity. Most involve the elements of novelty and usefulness. Often, to take full advantage of opportunities in a complex environment, ideas or solutions that constitute both novelty and usefulness are mandatory in order to remain competitive. If creativity in the workplace is desirable, how might it be achieved? Should strange yet creative "types" be hired to lock themselves away in a dark creative hole until an amazing new paradigm is accepted by all?

The organic truth is that an organization that employs personnel in any capacity is brimming with creative problem solvers or, in a more positive sense, creative opportunity seekers. Whether argument is for or against shades of Darwinism, every individual is engrained with creative potential. Organizations, however, may be lacking in the knowledge of effective methods designed to elucidate even the most fundamental processes of creativity.

Creative solutions to issues of complexity may be achieved via a systematic problem-solving approach. The key to effective problem solving is the discriminating use of divergent and convergent thinking modes. In short, unique solutions are rarely the first or second ideas on the table. The exercise of divergence via deferred judgment, freewheeling, seeking quantity, and piggybacking ideas is necessary to move through the ordinary toward desirable extraordinary solutions. Conversely, affirmative evaluation of potential solutions is also mandatory. In addition, convergence incorporates deliberateness, consideration of novelty, and attention to the ultimate objective.

Synapse Decisions (www.synapsedecisions.com) specializes in the training and facilitation of creative problem/opportunity-solving experiences. For example, a natural tendency in "brainstorming" sessions is to negate any new idea as soon as it is offered. We tend to find ourselves using the common phrase, "Yes, but ... " as a lead-in to an array of reasons why the idea is not feasible. In true divergent thinking sessions, idea generation is approached via a systematic process. All judgments are withheld until convergence is "officially" solicited. Knowledge and integration of the simple flow from divergence to convergence may significantly increase the effectiveness of time spent searching for novel and useful solutions.

In addition to the ability to recognize an effective creative problem-solving process in general, trained organization participants may assimilate a repertoire of specific tools designed to generate, evaluate, and implement ideas. For example, the idea-generation tool selection will be dependent upon the type of solution desired. If the objective is to produce a revolutionary or discreet option, "force fitting" environmental stimuli with the attributes of the opportunity at hand can be extremely useful. However, if you are looking for an evolutionary or incremental approach to the taming of complexity, a tool known as a "morphological matrix" may be beneficial. In this case the current area of interest is partitioned according to specific parameters. Potential changes in the whole are addressed one parameter at a time, resulting in a solution that is significantly different from, but overall similar to or recognizable as, its predecessor.

Current paradigms may not easily allow all necessary members of a solution-finding task force to meet face to face. However, people can use more sophisticated technology than the passing of thoughts and ideas via traditional e-mail. "E-storming," for instance, allows members to meet, by way of the Internet, asynchronously, i.e. at different places and different times as well as anonymously if necessary in order to develop and capture solutions to complex problems and/or opportunities.

Synapse Decisions offers a wide array of training and facilitation services designed to address the issues cited above, i.e. a) problem/opportunity identification; b) creative process development; c) idea generation, evaluation, and implementation; and d) "*e*-storming."

A SCIENTIFIC QUERY: QUESTIONING DARWIN'S HYPOTHESIS

Another extremely nice resource that offers a systems thinking alternative to dealing with complexity may be found at www.systemsthinkingpress.com. It provides some excellent articles as well as other resources.

There are three Websites that represent superbly the view standing in opposition to the Darwinian presupposition. The first is www.answersingenesis.org. This site has some excellent information, and the organization's resources are extremely good. However, the site does not offer a lot of links for the researcher.

The Institute for Creation Research may be found at www.icr.org. This site is run by people who hold a Judeo-Christian world view, but at the same time they approach the topic in a remarkably sterile manner and make every effort to avoid fallacious presuppositions. The site is rich with resources and features numerous articles and research by scientifically credible scholars. It is an exceptionally good site.

Phillip Johnson (mentioned earlier in this chapter) is a respected attorney and professor of law at UC Berkeley, CA. A number of years ago he grew interested in the field of evolution. Ultimately, he became convinced that the Darwinian hypothesis lacked credible support in the field of science. Over the years, he has written numerous books and articles on the topic. His Website is at www.arn.org.

While the three previous resources disagree with the Darwinian hypothesis (as do I), it would seem that those on both sides of the issue want to explore all the evidence related to a position in order to maintain researcher credibility. Further, "truth" is not determined by the observer. Truth exists independent of the observer's opinion. The law of noncontradiction reveals that there is no such thing as "contradictory truths." Or, as the famous baseball player Dizzy Dean once said, "It ain't braggin' if you can do it."

Those who presuppose pluralism (there may be multiple contradictory truths about any topic) do not belong in research. The researcher needs to have the ability to approach any topic without bias. At the same time, any researcher will readily admit that they continually deal with researcher bias. It is just that those who take their task seriously will make sure that they consider all sides of an issue to ensure integrity for the research.

That is the point of including resources that might disagree with the generally accepted view. From a scientific standpoint, there is significantly more evidence on the side of those who do not hold to the Darwinian hypothesis. As I stated earlier, if those individuals are correct, the Darwinian hypothesis may not be an effective metaphor upon which to base organizational theory.

In either case, to propose that organizations must "self organize" if they are to effectively confront complexity, or that the leadership of learning, transformation, and performance is most appropriate, both views should be considered. Without true academic honesty, which considers both views without bias, the selection of either view would be little more than blind faith.

Ten Steps to Making Complexity Work

What would be the value of a theory if it could not be used? This chapter offers specific steps that can be taken to enable a company to effectively handle complexity.

One of the dichotomies of the field of complexity in the business world involves the issue of developing a system for dealing with complexity. Left alone to "self organize," a business system will rapidly deteriorate into a politically based bureaucracy. That is the "black hole" that exists in the theoretical construct of most who propose self-organization and emergence as a method for dealing with complexity. The real world simply does not support that view (a great test for ideas, the real world).

I recently had the opportunity to meet the vice-chairman of one of the world's most successful companies in its industry. After listening to him talk about the history of the firm for almost an hour, one thing became apparent to me. The company had been through a number of CEOs and had endured a number of paradigm shifts over its history of almost 40 years. Each time the company had prevailed. The reason? Through the entire process, the vice-chairman (he had held numerous positions within the firm) had been there to carefully guide the company and keep it on track, even during some significant shifts in the global competitive environment.

Let us agree that most if not all companies in the global marketplace are dealing with complex dynamic systems (environments). At the same time, we do not see "leaderless" organizations doing well. Underlying success, as in the case of the company I cite above, is a purposeful, empowering, iconoclastic leader who wakes up every day with just two objectives: maximize today and maximize tomorrow ... today. Leaders create learning organizations. It is that simple.

In studying companies from around the world, I have come to one conclusion: success is never an accident. It is the result of insightful leadership. With that in mind, the ten steps below appear to be what those successful leaders create in their organizations.

WHY COMPANIES WIN

Over the past five years, I have had the opportunity to study some of the most successful companies in the world. In a number of cases, I met the CEO. In most instances, the company was one that had competed in a highly turbulent environment for a number of years. As the process of interviewing the different executives progressed, I began to see a distinct yet common pattern of behavior among all the CEOs. Certainly, each CEO was different, but in the end they all appeared to share a similar mental model of competition.

Gary Hamel and C.K. Prahalad discovered that the average CEO spends 97% of his or her time on operational issues.[1] I believe there are three types of CEOs: controllers, maintainers, and creators.[2] Controllers tend to be self-focused and punish creativity and risk taking. Maintainers see their job as sustaining the status quo, so they see no need for out-of-the-box behavior. Creators, on the other hand, insist that the company should be a learning organization. They are equally focused on performance and future profit. They value creativity and have little appreciation for those who focus on the organization's historic competencies. They are all about creating the future.

There is one other thing that I have observed in organizations that engage in long-term reinvention. Rather than focusing on the bottom line, they focus on *the behaviors that produce profitability*. This is where many get lost in the pursuit of profit. It is not the goal of being profitable that makes a company profitable. Everyone has that goal. It is those exceptional leaders who understand the contribution of each aspect of the complex organization who create sustainable performance.

Creators understand the necessity of managing the firm as a complex entity that is competing in a complex, dynamic environment. The following ten steps or behaviors are those that I have observed consistently at companies that thrive in complex environments. The key is not that they do just one or two of these things, but that they generally do all of them.

1. THE CEO

The first characteristic in successful companies is always the CEO.[3] In most instances of corporate failure in complex environments, the CEO (and executive team) is clearly at fault.[4] Simply put, success starts at the top of the organization. So does failure. This obviously flies in the face of the approach of self-organization proponents. As we have noted previously, reality (and the literature) simply does not support the idea in practice. (See also "The reinvention roller coaster" by Tracy Goss, Richard Pascale, and Anthony Athos in the Nov – Dec 1993 *Harvard Business Review*.) The bottom line is that the senior executive of the organization is critical in establishing a foundation for effectively dealing with complexity.

This reality is exemplified on a daily basis in the global marketplace. Companies that were in a downward spiral suddenly reinvent themselves. What happened? In almost every case, the firm changed its CEO by replacing a controller or maintainer-type CEO with a creator type. These CEOs, like Lou Gerstner of IBM, do not come to their jobs with a "get back to core business" mentality. Across the board, they find they must rekindle the company's entrepreneurial spirit in order to change its prospects. Again, great CEOs do not focus on profit, they focus on the behaviors that produce profitability.

2. AN ICONOCLASTIC MENTALITY

The second key is to establish an iconoclastic mentality across the entire organization. Iconoclastic behavior, or "challenging tradition," is a difficult thing for some managers to deal with, especially at the senior executive level. However, extremely successful executives (and managers) expect subordinates to challenge everything, including them. As we have noted previously in this book, the leaders at Microsoft Corporation foster a "challenge everything" attitude to ensure that the company continually adapts to environmental jolts.

In a lot of companies, employees are rewarded for compliance and "staying in the box." In linear environments that are characterized by high levels of predictability (and therefore, few surprises), compliance-based reward systems will work. In more turbulent environments, such approaches become a formula for failure.

In 1994, I gave a graduate research team the task of analyzing telecoms group AT&T and predicting the firm's profit. The team used only externally available data to conduct their assessment. The research revealed that AT&T had become a bureaucracy that rewarded linear thinking and compliance. As a result, the team predicted that the firm would not do well in the turbulent, complex times of the late 1990s unless major changes were made. By 2001, AT&T had deteriorated substantially. The Lucent spin-off proved equally disastrous. The firm proved that its people (especially the leaders) were unable to change their mental models in order to deal with the new complexity of the millennium. They found it impossible to engage in iconoclastic behavior. Rather than changing the competitive profile of each division of the firm so that they would be capable of performing in complex environments, they somehow thought that spinning them off would help their competitiveness. This is tantamount to changing the oil in an automobile that has run out of gasoline and will not run.

3. TRAINING

The *third* aspect of dealing with complexity is training. There are two types of training that normally occur: formal and informal. Informal training takes place on the job. It is the result of encouragement and direction from superiors as well as co-workers that reveals the corporate commitment to reinvention and creativity. A lot of companies talk about how they listen to their employees, but few act on the idea. In fact when workers find themselves employed at a company that really does encourage iconoclastic behavior, they may have problems adjusting. Often, new employees go through a "cultural shock" period when they find that their employer continually reaffirms the value of creativity and "out of the box" thinking.

There are a number of ways that companies engage in formal complexity training. As we stated earlier, Nortel Networks developed a training program for senior managers that was implemented on a global basis. Every manager was trained in the field of complexity, and especially how it impacted their ability to do their job.

A lot of companies send their managers to "systems thinking" conferences. Some of these conferences feature training and exercises that are extremely beneficial in providing managers with systems thinking tools to help them deal with complexity. In reality, systems thinking is the key to developing an effective approach for dealing with complexity.

As we mentioned earlier, the training offered by Synapse Decisions has been extremely well received. Rather than suggest a single solution to training needs in this area, all three of the above tools should be considered.

4. VALUING EMPLOYEES

The fourth aspect or key to dealing with complexity focuses on how a company values its people. The ability to value every member of a team, and to clearly act on that value, is the foundation for any system of dealing with complexity. Trust is an important component of value.

The purpose of a complexity program is to pool the intellectual capital or knowledge of the entire company, the point of which is obvious. The problem involves getting levels of trust as well as enthusiasm for sharing knowledge to develop. Great leaders understand that they are nothing without access to the combined knowledge of the whole organization. At the same time, if condescending, controlling behavior is tolerated on the part of managers, there will be no upward flow of knowledge. That is why great leaders value their people. They spend a great deal of time in communicating that value. They award and recognize people who take risks, are creative, and share knowledge with the organization.

Sharing, however, must be built on trust and integrity. At one organization, a senior manager developed a habit of constantly seeking the input of subordinates. He was a great listener, and encouraged such sharing. He then took the subordinates' ideas and shared them with the CEO of the firm as if they were his own. As a result, his subordinates lost trust in him because they did not feel he had the integrity to accurately attribute ideas to their true author. Within a short time, the senior executive had no more ideas because his people were unwilling to share with him.

Companies like Southwest Airlines never experience a shortage of ideas and knowledge because they continually communicate the value they place on their people. At Southwest Airlines, there are 300 applicants for every job that comes up. Should that surprise anyone?

5. MANAGEMENT TOOLS

The fifth key to managing complexity has to do with the management tools that a company employs. If changing mental models has to do with an individual's ability to deal with environmental change and discontinuities, solutions may be difficult to find. Two tools can be extremely valuable in helping people change the way they think about issues.

The first is scenarios. A lot of companies effectively use scenarios to help them plan for an uncertain future. Scenarios involve a process of creating a set of possible futures, based upon an analysis of key forces.

Once the different scenarios are created, they are ranked from most probable to least probable. In addition to helping the manager to better understand the future environment, scenarios are excellent learning tools in that they help managers deal with bias issues.

The second tool for dealing with uncertainty and complexity is war gaming. In war gaming, different teams are formed and each team takes on the role of one of the competitors in the target market. In most cases, each team is given research about the company they are representing so they can try to emulate the company's behavior. The teams then go through competitive cycles. First, each team prepares a strategic plan and presents it to all the others. Once they hear the other teams' competitive moves, each team regathers and develops a new strategy to address what they have just heard. This may be repeated a number of times. War gaming can be extremely effective in helping a firm's managers not only to anticipate competitors' moves but also to develop an effective strategic plan to deal with the anticipated complexity of the market.

6. ORGANIZATIONAL STRUCTURE

The sixth key to dealing with complexity has to do with organizational structure. As environments become more complex, and especially as the rate of environmental change accelerates, highly flexible formal structures become necessary. At moderately high levels of change and complexity, matrix structures can significantly increase the speed and flexibility of organizational responses. A matrix involves the combination of a functional structure with cross-functional/cross-product relationships. This might mean that a sales person might have a direct responsibility to the sales manager, but that the individual might also be involved in a product development project simultaneously. Numerous combinations of such cross-relationships are possible. Regardless of whether the supporting leadership and culture are present, the matrix structure can really help in dealing with complexity.

At higher levels of change and complexity, bicentralized organizational structures may be added to the matrix format. At higher levels of turbulence (complexity and rate of change), speed is of the essence. Thus, a bicentralized organization that creates dual power centers is important. What this means is that significant levels of power rest in the senior executive team, while at the same time each product division is highly empowered to act somewhat independently. This type of power structure creates a high-speed, adaptive organization.

7. REWARDS AND RECOGNITION

The seventh key involves rewards and recognition. H. Edwards Deming, the founder of the TQM (total quality management) movement, once said that "what gets done is what gets inspected." When it comes to creating high levels of creativity, risk taking, and entrepreneurial activity, appropriate rewards and recognition must be developed. Often companies recognize the need to increase the level of their organizational aggressiveness in response to increased levels of environmental turbulence, but they fail to recognize that rewards and incentives must also be changed to ensure that the new behavior is created. Notice also that rewards without recognition have little benefit in creating sustainable performance.

8. PEOPLE ASSETS

The eighth key involves people assets. Some people, regardless of how academically qualified they are, are just not suited for positions that involve extremely high levels of creativity or risk taking. Some are much more resistant to change than others, and further, a person's innate resistance to change is not variable. It is fixed. (Again, see my article "Making the break: from competitive analysis to strategic intelligence," *Competitive Intelligence Review*, 1995, John Wiley and Sons, New York, NY.)

Insightful managers understand that there are different types of "learning" personalities. Therefore they are smart enough to identify their natural "learners" and put them into key learning roles. At the same time, they also understand that they need to segregate high-resistance personalities away from critical learning activities.

9. FORMAL INTELLIGENCE FUNCTION

The ninth key involves the use of a formal intelligence function within the organization. Intelligence is the systematic gathering and analysis of information about competitors or other factors that could impact an organization. For a number of reasons, the intelligence function needs to be formalized in a company. In some cases, companies attempt to add the intelligence process into other jobs, but this is generally unsuccessful. An intelligence organization needs to be staffed by intelligence professionals.

The intelligence function needs to report directly to the senior executive of the firm. There are two reasons for establishing that relationship. First, the information needs to get to the person who has the power to act. That necessitates the reporting relationship to the CEO. Second, if the intelligence team reports directly to the CEO, it minimizes the "filter effect" on the information. Managers, for the purpose of avoiding accountability or to hide a personal failure, often filter undesirable information to keep it from the CEO. Sometimes it is simply a matter of the potential loss of power. In the long run such filtering can damage the organization.

10. PLANNING MODEL

The tenth issue or step in the process of dealing with complexity has to do with the planning model that the company uses. As of 2001 most companies are still using a linear planning model (core competencies, mission, vision, competitive advantage). It makes little sense to use a linear model in planning for a nonlinear environment. Complex environments by definition are nonlinear.

If a company is to operate well in a complex environment, it is constantly involved in a dynamic cycle of transformation. Earlier, we gave the definition of management for complex environments: "Management is the leading of organizational learning, transformation, and performance." That means that an organization is continually focusing upon maximizing what it is, what it is becoming (for the near term), and what it will need to become in the future. Complexity demands that all three processes are ongoing.

The Ansoff model[5] is the only truly holistic strategic model that fits the nonlinear requirement. People who intuitively understand how to accomplish a similar process lead a lot of companies, but the only formalized process is the Ansoff model itself. Also, it is important to remember that as environmental complexity increases and rates of environmental change accelerate, the Ansoff model prescribes the use of other tools such as scenarios.

THE BOTTOM LINE

It would be incorrect to suggest that the ten "steps" I have been discussing will work if carried out one at a time. It may be appropriate to institute an effective complexity system into an organization by initiating each process individually, but in the end it is important for all ten processes to be simultaneous and continual.

Companies that handle complexity well are those that dynamically renew. In spite of economic downturns, or even mistakes, they are continually striving for leadership in their chosen competitive arenas. Most importantly, companies that handle complexity well make substantially higher profits than those that do not. That is the bottom line of complexity and profit.

NOTES

1 Hamel, Gary and Prahalad, C.K. (1994) *Seeing the Future First*, The Harvard Business School Press, Boston, MA.

2 Underwood, James (2001) "Beware of your firm's core competencies," *Competia Magazine* (www.competia.com), September 3.

3 See *Thriving in E-Chaos* (Underwood, James D. (2001) Prima Publishers, Roseville, CA) for a complete explanation of CEO attributes.

4 Tushman, Michael L., Newman, William H., and Romanelli, Elaine (1986) "Convergence and upheaval: managing the unsteady pace of organizational evolution," *California Management Review*, Vol. XXIX, No. 1, Fall.

5 See *Thriving in E-Chaos*, Chapter 2.

Frequently Asked Questions (FAQs)

Q1: What is complexity?

A: Complexity is a term that has been passed around between a wide range of disciplines from information technology to biology. Complexity refers to the almost infinite number of individual "systems" that exist in the global or world system, or within the universe as a system.

Q2: Isn't this the same as chaos theory?

A: Complexity and chaos theory are first cousins. Chaos theory simply refers to the chaotic or unpredictable manner in which elements of a system may interact, such as the molecules in water.

Q3: What is Darwin's theory of evolution?

A: Darwin's "theory" is actually a hypothesis. A theory is a hypothesis that has research supporting it. Darwin hypothesized that the world was not created but came to be by chance. He also proposed that in nature, through natural selection and upward mutations, all life forms were continually improving. At this point in time, there is no evidence to elevate his hypothesis to theory status.

Q4: What is the equilibrium theory of economics and how did it come to be the basis for a lot of management theories?

A: Equilibrium theory has been the foundation for most of the management theories that have been developed over the past century or so. Economist David Ricardo came up with the idea of "comparative advantage." That led to ideas like "competitive advantage" and "core competencies." This is a linear approach to management which assumes that the future will be repetitive of the past.

Q5: What about the proposed alternative to equilibrium theory called "complex adaptive systems?"

A: Complex adaptive systems is a blending of complex systems theory (including chaos theory) and Darwin's hypothesis.

Q6: How did Darwin's hypothesis (theory) get adapted to complexity?

A: A common practice in many fields is to use ideas or mental models from other fields to explain phenomena. Since Charles Darwin first put his hypothesis forward, the idea has been used metaphorically in many fields, including theology and business.

Q7: Does the problem with Darwin's ideas mean that complexity theory is not useful?

A: Not at all, it just means that we need to look at complexity in a slightly different way. Complex dynamic systems may be a better way to look at the issue. The global system has order, yet there are numerous complex systems that make future events highly unpredictable.

Q8: Why is this stuff important to me as a manager?

A: There are two reasons. First, complexity is reality. As a manager, you need to know how to manage in complex environments. Second, there are some assumptions that are being forced into complexity theory that have no basis in fact. It is important for a manager to know what works and what doesn't.

Q9: Can this help me be a better manager?

A: Research shows that managers who understand the complexity and rate of change in the environment are more effective (profit wise) than those who do not.

Q10: This all sounds so technical. How can I understand it?

A: A lot of books on the topic are written in highly technical terms. We have tried to present the material in this book in a clear, understandable way.

Index